Adventures in Global Selling

Adventures in Global Selling

Gayle Hickok

and

Bill Wilson

RED ANVIL BOOKS

RED ANVIL BOOKS
is an imprint of
ELDERBERRY PRESS, INC.
1393 Old Homestead Drive
Oakland OR 97462

RED ANVIL BOOKS are available from your favorite bookstore, amazon.com, or from the Elderberry Press 24 hour order line: 1.800.431.1579

Library of Congress Control Number: 2010930593
Publisher's Catalog-in-Publication Data
Adventures In Global Selling/ Gayle Hickok and Bill Wilson

ISBN-13: 978-1-934956-34-2
ISBN-10: 1-934956-34-1
1. Sales.
2. Adventure.
3. Russia.
4. Politics.
5. Beakup of the Soviet Union.
I. Title

This book was written, printed and bound in the United States of America.

CONTENTS

A Note to the Reader

This book is Gayle Hickok's story.
We have written it in the first person.

Introduction

The book you are about to read began a few years ago. One evening Gayle and Bill and some friends were enjoying a meal and a night out at a restaurant near La Paz on Mexico's beautiful Baja peninsula.

Gayle asked Bill, "How would you like to collaborate on a book about my adventures, a book that would also include lessons from my experiences?" Bill replied, "Let's do it, the idea's a great one." That's how this book began. Bill's interviews with Gayle form the book's backbone. It's fleshed out here and there with other sources, but the judgments are always Gayle's. We think we've achieved a nice balance between recounting Gayle's amazing adventures and drawing sales and marketing methods from them.

Each of us takes full responsibility for what you find here. That doesn't mean we could have done the book on our own. We had a lot of help from others and we want to thank them for it.

Thanks to Kitty Wilson for her editorial skills.

Thanks to Sukey Janes for drawing that "gate selling" diagram.

Special thanks to Jess Kellogg for giving us a lot to write about.

Thanks to Dave St. John and the staff at Elderberry Press.

Thanks to everyone else who made it all happen.

Gayle Hickok
Bill Wilson

Chapter One

Introducing This Book

It was a bright, sunny day in July 1974. I was driving my new Maserati from my Toronto office east to the one in Montreal with my daughter Lisa, then a pert twelve year old but, you know, mentally going on thirty. We were cruising comfortably at a steady 100 mph, when I began a lecture on one of the several subjects that we single dads and their growing daughters have to deal with. The theme of my lectures was almost always the same, how growing daughters should benefit from the accumulated wisdom of their dads.

Lisa knew we were strapped in and she had no place of escape for at least three hours. I'd just launched my lecture when she interrupted.

"Hold it, hold it," she commanded. "Wait a minute. I need to make you a deal."

"What do you mean, make me a deal," I asked. "I'm the boss here."

"Well," she went on, "you can just tell me the end of your lecture and I'll let you know if I need to hear the beginning and the middle." She was right, I admit, because she'd heard precisely the same thing many times before. After that, we had only condensed versions of our little talks, with an emphasis on fast forwarding to the focus of our discussion.

That conversation in my speeding coupe was just one more proof of the fact that we adults learn from our children, as I certainly have from all five of mine. Now I'm learning from my grandkids. I'm going to apply some of that knowledge by making three points with you.

• • •

First point: In keeping with Lisa's concept, I'm going to begin my story with the ending, at least as my life has developed so far. I hope from that you'll decide to explore the beginning and the middle with me.

• • •

Second point: I'm a professional salesman, through and through, and damn proud of it. Oh, yes, I've been the manager, owner, vice-president, even president of various business ventures, but the highest compliment you can pay me is "You sure are a good salesman." I've had fun selling. I love selling because it has opened me to new and exciting experiences.

Another thing. I highly respect sales people of both genders, but please excuse me for not referring to folks in our profession as "salespersons." I love women. They are some of the best in the business. But "salesperson" is a clumsy word. After all, Arthur Miller didn't name his famous play "Death of a Salesperson." Sometimes "person" just doesn't apply. I remember how the town of Woonsocket, Rhode Island was ridiculed after it renamed manholes "personholes" and manhole covers "personhole covers." So I'll refer to "people in sales" or "sales people" at times but always to myself as a "salesman."

• • •

Third point: Throughout my story I've sprinkled anecdotes and incidents which I hope will entertain you. Often I'll be describing sales situations which illustrate an important lesson that I've learned, either from others or through my own experiences. Don't worry, this isn't another one of those hundreds of "how-to" volumes or "salesmanship" workbooks. My purpose is to stimulate, inform, and inspire you, and if I do those things, I'll be really pleased that together we've accomplished something meaningful and worthwhile.

Chapter Two

Introducing Gayle

I'm a salesman. I'm beginning at what for now is the end of my selling story and I'll tell it to you in one short paragraph.

I've worked and lived all over the world, and now I'm working and living in the best place on the planet, the La Paz area of Mexico's Baja California peninsula. I'm working for a first-rate development company, Lomas del Centenario. Here the air is clear and bright, the temperature is moderate for most of the year, the people are friendly, and the crime rate is low. By a little luck and some design, I arrived here several years ago and doubt I'll ever leave.

Now then, find out who I am and how I got here. As I've told you, the highest compliment anyone can pay me is, "You're a great salesman!" This book is about how and why I became a successful salesman and cheerfully gave my adult life to selling. You should read it because you and I are alike, we are in sales, along with everybody else. You think, wait a minute, I'm a teacher or a housewife or a doctor or any other occupation light years away from selling. In fact we are all selling.

Let's face it, teachers are selling themselves and their subject matter to their students. Housewives are selling their husbands on repainting the living room and their kids on taking out the trash. Doctors are selling treatments to their patients. Employers, if they want to keep their employees, are selling themselves to their workforce. Employees, regardless of whether they want to stay with their employers or use their present jobs as stepping stones to other work, are marketing themselves to their employers.

It's only when some of us become professional sellers that other people set us apart as folks who aren't quite legitimate. Trust me, I've heard all the jokes, the jibes, and the stories about sales people. They make the male of the species out to be pudgy, pushy, and a blusterer. He's dressed in a loud checked yellow jacket, a rumpled bright green shirt, brown houndstooth slacks ending about two inches above his ankles, argyle socks, and scuffed tan loafers with frayed tassels.

If this clown wears a tie it's a bold pattern splotched with this morning's breakfast. If he knows more than the minimum about the product he's selling it's an accident. Often he's less than truthful about what he does know, because he's too absorbed in making a quick buck, and then moving on to the real business of his life, fast cars, boozing, and chasing women. Our stereotype guy isn't very bright or well educated. He mangles grammar, recycles a limited vocabulary, and mouths clichés, "Right," or "You bet, baby."

There may be, probably are, salesmen like the stereotype. If they are successful it's in spite of their appearance and attitude. If they are successful it's because they use selling methods that work. I'm successful partly because I don't dress or act like the stereotype, but mostly because I and other consistent producers use proven methods. I repeat, this isn't a methods book, though I'll share with you some successful selling techniques and methods along the way. I pull together these methods under the heading of nine "Be's" later on.

• • •

I'm really irked by the notion that people in sales are dim bulbs. That is not my experience with other people in sales. They are at least as intelligent, thoughtful, and well educated as the general population. Speaking for myself, I've written course outlines and notes, sales brochures, and other promotional pieces. I'm the author of the pamphlet, "The Five Myths of Mexican Real Estate," which we distribute at our Lomas del Centenario company seminars in the United States and Canada. Later I'll give you a condensed version of that pamphlet, my explanation of what Mexico really is, versus the "bandido" and drug-infested image promoted in the media.

I'm the author of a TV documentary script on the global crisis of overpopulation. I argued that unchecked population growth caused or worsened all the dangers bedeviling the experts. I related climate change, food shortages, the lack of clean water, soil depletion, the pressure on natural resources, and the conversion of cropland to housing to the need for population control.

I didn't endorse coercive population control like China's but appealed to enlightened self-interest. The script is complete with voice-over dialogue and descriptions of visuals. I wrote it during one of those rare instances in my life when I had some free time and friends in the TV production industry. But I got busy again and never submitted it. In any case the script demonstrates my literacy, and my concern for issues beyond booze, women, and fancy cars. Many people in sales share those concerns.

• • •

Besides a knack for writing, I have the ability and ambition to operate successful businesses. Some I ran myself, others in partnership. Other companies demonstrated respect for my ability by hiring me as a consultant. I liked all those experiences, but they took me away from my first love, selling. I always wanted to return to selling. Whatever I do in the future, I'm determined to allow time and space to be on the front line in sales.

Selling is not just about selling, it's about opening doors to other adventures and experiences. Look at my life. I've had the wonderful opportunity of traveling all over the world and I've actually lived in Canada, Mexico, the Cayman Islands, England, Australia, Thailand, Russia, the Bahamas, and, of course, all around the United States. I've sold Fords, car washes, video games, country club memberships, houses, condos, timeshares, car wash franchises, modular homes, and tire recycling plants. I've even sold scientists who possessed dangerous skills on the idea of retiring rather than letting their knowledge fall into the wrong hands. In addition to being a consultant, I've been a motivational speaker described as a "walking enthusiasm generator." My real estate sales course taught at least one member of the class "more in one day than all four years of selling experience."

If success is measured by the accumulation of this world's goods, I have my share. I own a respectable amount of real estate, and I have all the toys most men would want. Did I manage to get all this – debt free, in case you're wondering – by treading the miser's path to accumulation? Not on your life! I've always spent money to make a sale, have fun, or enjoy creature comforts. At one time during what I call my "look at me, baby" phase, I owned two Maseratis, a good thing because one or the other was always in the shop, and a Rolls Royce. Expensive suits were my trademark. Cheap hotels and apartments held no charms for me, and I went high-end as soon as I found my financial feet.

• • •

Far beyond material goods, I value my family. I have a wonderful younger sister, Claudia, who lives in Palm Springs, California. Two marriages blessed me with five children. All of them are grown, and I have watched their development with loving interest over the years. Deborah, my oldest, is married to Phil, a successful realtor and the author of real estate sales books. Scott, my second oldest son, and his wife work with Deborah and Phil in the real estate business. Edward, my oldest son, has been an excellent salesman, too, and now lives with his wife in Hawaii. Steven, the youngest son, lives with his wife in Montana, where he works for Wal-Mart. Lisa, a housewife for most of her adult life, lives in Oregon. All together they've presented me with eleven grandchildren, and the grandkids have produced two great grandchildren. So I've made my contribution to the propagation of the race! And I'm not done yet!

I'm a contented man, not because of my possessions, or even because of my family. Success has made me happy, but what is success? Here it is: success is the progressive realization of meaningful, worthwhile goals. You can be as successful as I am, or more successful than I, by setting a series of worthwhile goals and moving toward them. Read what I have to say later about this program, then consistently, persistently apply the techniques I present there, and you will succeed. When you succeed in the way I'll present, you will have something more precious than riches, and that's peace of mind. That's what success in life will produce, peace of mind.

Let me repeat this. Success in all the important areas of life will come to people who diligently move toward commendable, constructive goals. Sellers who succeed are almost always ordinary people doing extraordinary things because they have learned how to motivate themselves. Does having peace of mind free them from the minor irritations of life? No, but they realize that the irritations are minor and easily dealt with. Does success mean that they became perfect? No. Does my success make me perfect? Hardly. But I have worked hard to improve my approach to sales, as well as enrich other areas of my life. As a result I love selling more and more every day.

How much do I love selling? I've retired twice, grown colossally bored or mentally itchy in a few months, and returned to selling both times. I'm trying to retire again, to my new house with a smashing view of a lovely bay in Mexico. Will it work this time? We'll see, but if selling lures me again, don't be surprised. As I told you at the beginning, the highest compliment anyone can pay me is "You're a great salesman."

• • •

Now a final word before we look at my life. I've had many adventures. Most of them were hugely rewarding, while some were memorable even without any financial or psychic gain, and one or two were terrifying, such as watching a friend's head blown apart by a pistol shot. I tell all of them as I remember them. Someone else who was there could remember those incidents a little differently. I will tell these stories my way because it's my life, the life of a salesman.

Chapter Three

Getting Started in Making Big Sales

If you're wondering when I began selling, keep reading. Before I could sell anything I had to be born, in Terry, Montana, in 1934. Terry is a small town on the Yellowstone River in eastern Montana, in fact the Yellowstone is on the north side, and now Interstate 94 is on the south side. Other than being the county seat and my birthplace, the only other thing Terry had to recommend it was where my father, Thomas, worked at my grandfather's Ford agency. My father was a car mechanic, or as we would say nowadays, a technician.

I want to pause just for a moment to introduce you to my grandfather, Claude Wagner, a wonderful, talented man. Granddad gave me the inspiration, the security, and the helping hand up that even the best of us need at least once in our lives. He could help financially because he made a great success of that Ford agency.

You'd think that Terry would be too small to support a stand-alone, single make dealership. When I was born the Great Depression was going full blast and a Ford agency in a fairly isolated place like Terry was one of the few money makers around. Granddad's agency dated from the days of the Ford Model T, the greatest all-time sales maker for one model until the original Volkswagen beetle finally beat its record. Model T sales slowed in the later 1920s, so Ford followed the Model T with the Model A in 1928. The A was an extremely popular car until the really hard times came in 1931.

Then Ford produced the first low-priced V-8 for the 1932 model year. It was a marvel of power and speed, and sold despite the Great Depression. The V-8 was such a hot car the gangsters loved it. John Dillinger, the FBI's Public Enemy Number One for a time in the 1930s wrote Henry Ford, "Hello Old Pal. You have a wonderful car. It's a treat to drive one." Clyde Barrow, the notorious outlaw of Bonnie and Clyde fame, went Dillinger one better. He wrote Ford about how "I have drove Fords exclusively when I could get away with one." Barrow's statement wouldn't pass muster with the grammarians but he got his point across. So Granddad's agency handled three of the hottest automotive sellers in a row. His location and his ability paid off for him.

Back then, people stayed loyal to their local dealer. They almost had to. People thought highways were great if they were graveled and had two-lane bridges. You just didn't wander fifty or a hundred miles from home to buy a car, because most roads weren't good enough and the low-priced cars, at least, weren't that comfortable. Most people worked long hours and didn't have the time, so if you had to have some repair work done that you couldn't do yourself, you went to the nearest dealership.

With twenty or twenty-five percent of the workforce unemployed and many of the employed working for peanuts, most people couldn't afford a new car. The Great Depression forced a lot of folks to keep their Model Ts or Model As, or other old cars long after they would have traded them. Granddad made money on his service department, keeping those old cars running, even when new car sales slowed.

• • •

World War II saved me from growing up in Terry. My parents – my mother was Alice Hickok – moved in 1942 to Missoula, Montana, briefly, then to what was a little, forested town, Woodinville, not far from Seattle. They were shipyard workers in nearby Kirkland, a Seattle suburb that looks west into the city from across Lake Washington.

After the war my dad became something of a rolling stone. We moved to Port Angeles, on Washington State's Olympic Peninsula. Then we lived in Sequim (pronounced Skwim), near Port Angeles, then back to Port Angeles as Dad worked at different mechanic's jobs. I bounced around from school to school but got through a year of high school before Mom split from Dad.

Then we – my Mom, sister, and I – moved in with my maternal

grandfather. By then he had sold his dealership in Montana but earned money from leasing the building and from his active commercial real estate agency. He specialized in apartments and business buildings. He had a nice house in the Hawthorne Hills section of northeast Seattle with enchanting views of Lake Washington and the Cascade Mountains. He was really the major father figure of my life. For years he drilled into my head, "Go buy corner lots in growing cities," and "you gotta go into real estate. Go to the University of Washington, study business administration, learn all you can about real estate."

Granddad's enthusiasm and purpose in life were responsible, ultimately, for my life in real estate sales. He was an outgoing guy, an outdoorsman who made hunting and fishing trips to Alaska. He was a dedicated patriot who flew the flag on national holidays, but was too old for the service when World War II began. He wanted to do something for his country so he closed his real estate business and took a job as a uniformed guard at Boeing aircraft, where they produced the great B-17 bomber. He was proud of that uniform. After the war he reopened his real estate business.

Now you're thinking, this is where Gayle goes into sales and makes his millions, if he isn't making them already. I'd like to tell you that was true, or that I just needed a little grandfatherly advice to get off my newspaper route into something bigger. I'd like to tell you stories similar to those in some salesmen's autobiographies, for instance that I was selling before I could walk. Would you believe that I took the sheets off my crib mattress and sold them to expectant moms in Terry? No? How about my standing on a street corner at age four hawking the *Saturday Evening Post* in deep snow while a Montana blizzard howled around me? Or that I was such a super salesman that I repeatedly sold out and ran barefoot through the snowdrifts for more magazines? Huh?

I thought so. Sales had to wait awhile. I graduated from Roosevelt High School, north of Seattle's University District, in 1952. Then I entered the University of Washington, majoring in business administration. Anyone who went to the University of Washington with me in the years 1952 to 1955 who returns to the campus today discovers more change than continuity. Most former students on the "upper campus" will orient themselves on the magnificent Collegiate Gothic façade of the Suzzallo Library.

The original Suzzallo is much the same but the cool, green plaza in front is gone, replaced by a red brick paving on top of a vast underground parking garage, today's "Red Square." Blocky buildings enclose "Red Square," covering much of what was open space then.

In my day Collegiate Gothic buildings dominated the campus. Many of them went up in the teens, twenties, and thirties. Sure, there were a few buildings in contemporary styles but they didn't compete for architectural control as they later did.

The feel of the campus was more spacious, relaxed, and at the same time more intimate. The intimacy wasn't because of the many fewer buildings. There were only about 16,000 of us students, compared to more than 40,000 now. I couldn't have imagined that kind of growth in the intervening years.

Not many of us concerned ourselves with the university's prestige. I certainly didn't. I was a local boy going to the nearest local university and that was about it. In 2008 the university made much over its ranking of 11th among the national public universities in the *U.S. News and World Report* ratings. It didn't move up in the 2009 rankings, so scarcely mentioned them. It did celebrate its second place in the Sierra Club's list of environmentally conscious universities. Greenopia put it on the top of the heap among the "greenest" universities, another cause for celebration. Ratings like that didn't exist in my day and I doubt that they would have made much difference to me if they had.

In any case I wasn't a joiner or a big man on campus. Working my way through the university took too much time. By then Granddad had taught me how to play the piano, a skill I supplemented by reading and applying books on chords and practice exercises. My piano playing helped to pay my way through the university. I formed a trio with two classmates, a bass fiddle player and a drummer, and we played calm, gentle, "old ladies" type music for the luncheon meetings of a women's club. Old ladies! I'll bet I'm older now than most of the women were then! We thought of them as ancient but the perspective of young men changes as they age.

Music has always been part of my life from my piano playing days. I even enrolled in music appreciation while at the university, not your typical course for a major in business administration. Now I have a nice keyboard and play for parties with friends here in Mexico. But, to go back to my university days, I never graduated. I got married and had to get a job working in a supermarket.

• • •

The so-called Cold War with the Soviet Union and its allies was in full swing then, and I was a prime candidate for the military draft. I didn't evade the draft but avoided it because my wife and I began a family. In those days if your draft board had a good supply of young unmarried men or young men who were married but without children, the board called them first. The other thing I did was join the Navy Air Reserves at the Sand Point Naval Air Station on Lake Washington. The Navy could have called us up individually but it didn't.

I was an Airman First Class, not a bad rating, and I didn't have a bad job, but the job I did have convinced me that I wasn't made for a military career. I was the flight engineer, and sat between the pilot and co-pilot of our squadron's first aircraft, the PBY. It wasn't exactly flying first class and it wasn't meant to be. On one training exercise I had the flu and couldn't fly. Another airman took my place. On that exercise the pilot decided to shoot a water landing because he was tired of waiting for a long line of planes to land on the field. In anticipation of a field landing, he'd put the wheels down. Nobody, not the pilot, not the co-pilot, not the flight engineer, not the control tower, remembered or noticed that the landing gear was down. The wheels hit the water, pitched the plane forward, it sank, and the pilot, co-pilot, and flight engineer were killed.

We had a much more exciting but thank God not fatal episode after the squadron graduated to the PB 442, the Navy's version of the B-17. One time we were going out on a practice bombing with fifteen recruits on their first flight, tanks full of gas, and bays loaded with bombs. We'd just become airborne when the tower notified us that our starboard landing gear wasn't up. The hydraulic system had failed, and the landing gear was just flapping around loose.

I went back into the belly of the plane to try to crank the landing gear up manually but it wouldn't go. Now the problem is, if you try to come in on one good landing gear, the plane will tip, spin around, maybe even cartwheel. The only solution was to try for a belly landing, but first we had to fly out to Puget Sound, jettison our ammunition, and dump all our gas until we had just enough gas left to get back.

The pilot raised our good landing gear, knowing that the bad one would collapse on impact anyway. It was quite a show. We came in as low and slow as we dared. The ground crew laid down fire suppressant foam on the runway, the fire trucks and ambulances were out there, every emergency siren was wailing, and almost everybody at the station was lining the runway. We hit the runway, made a terrible grinding racket, but the plane stayed on the runway and there was no fire. Those fifteen recruits, mostly eighteen-year-olds, sure had a memorable first flight. They were scared green, which isn't to say that the rest of us considered it a picnic.

After that incident we refused to have the same number, 203, on our replacement plane but that didn't help us much. I wasn't on board for this one, but it was at least as big a deal because the plane landed just short of the runway and broke in two. Nobody was hurt but the ground crew was a good month cleaning up the wreckage. Our squadron was rather infamous. By the time of the third wreck I'd decided that the military life wasn't for me. I got out when my time was up.

• • •

At any event I was only what they called a "weekend warrior," and I needed more than the scanty air reserve pay and my income from clerking in a supermarket to raise a family. So I asked my uncle, Eugene Wagner, for a job in his Ford dealership in Burien, Washington. Burien is in the Seattle metro area, just south of Seattle. My uncle put me in the parts department where I worked for a time. There was nothing wrong with the parts department work, and I learned a lot about the complexities involved in keeping a car dealership functioning, not to mention keeping cars on the road. But a lot of it was routine and less than exciting.

My mind kept returning to what Granddad said about sales, not real estate sales especially, but selling in general. I remembered what my supermarket manager said, after watching me help customers and point out things they might buy.

"You know," he said, "you're a natural-born salesman."

As you'll discover later, I don't accept the belief about "natural born" salesmen. I think that anyone can sell if he or she has the right outlook and determination to succeed. In any case, I'd made it a point to be friendly to our customers. Conversations with those customers made me concerned with meeting their needs, insofar as I could do that with our supermarket stock. What was at least as important, I noticed that the salesmen who visited the supermarket were well dressed, self-assured types who obviously weren't leading a threadbare existence.

I went to the public library and read books on selling and watched some of the photo slide presentations on selling that they had there. The thing that really stayed with me was this: people rarely buy an object itself, be it a house, a car, or a coffeemaker. They buy objects that involve or project a style of life, a self image, or some life goal that they want to achieve. This reality has come home to me again and again. Like it or not, people don't buy, say, a house. They buy a "home" that, within their ability to pay, reflects and reinforces the way they live, or believe that they ought to live.

Armed with this insight, a lot of brassy nerve, and the eagerness of a twenty-two year old, I went to my uncle and asked him if I could go into sales. I told him I'd made up my mind to make selling my life's work. He said, "young people your age don't usually sell cars," but hesitantly and reluctantly he let me have a shot at it.

• • •

The car business has changed so much and so many times since I got into it that you have to understand what it was like in 1956. Back then, imports were, as they say, a cloud no bigger than a man's hand. One import segment was upscale, of the Rolls Royce and Bentley type, cars priced well beyond what almost everybody could pay. Then there was the low end, the Volkswagen end, made up of cramped, little, underpowered cars that weren't that much cheaper than a stripped down version of a much roomier Chevy, Ford, or (in those days) Plymouth. I don't think I'd even seen a Volkswagen then. When I did hear about them, what I heard about was their limited space, ugly shape, slow speed, and loud, unconventional air-cooled engines. They weren't to be taken seriously.

Practically all car buyers were wedded to one product family. They were Ford, General Motors, Chrysler buyers, or they bought independent makes not belonging to the Big Three. Oh, they might move up within a product line, trade up from a Ford to a Mercury or even a Lincoln, but they stayed in the line. There were a few independent makes around that survived the Great Depression and World War II, Studebaker, Packard, Hudson, Nash, Willys – but they were gone or going. Postwar startups like Kaiser faded pretty quickly. We didn't worry about them any more than we worried about imports.

Back then we could count on a Ford buyer having brand loyalty, returning to us at the Ford dealership to buy another Ford. Women rarely went into our stores, unless their husbands or some other man accompanied them. Despite that, we knew that women had a say in buying cars, for instance, in how much car the family could afford, in interior features such as easily adjustable seats, and in exterior and interior color combinations.

But the talk on the floor between sales staff and customer was usually man-to-man. There was some dickering over the price of the new car and over the trade-in allowance, but most of the man-to-man talk was about the engine or other mechanical features of the new car. When we did talk money, the talk was mostly about getting the monthly payments down to a level the customer would or could accept.

You may think that salesmen for the Big Three had an easier time of it then with no foreign competition and a high degree of brand loyalty. Also there were no professional bargainers hired to negotiate a price for the real buyer. *Consumer Reports* "New Car

Price Report" that reveals exactly what dealers pay for each car and each option, and how much they receive in cash rebates from the manufacturer, did not exist.

Personal technology opens up a whole new negotiating package for customers. Folks who don't subscribe to *Consumer Reports* or use its website can search for detailed information on their Blackberrys and iPhones. Using Twitter, a customer can ask fellow Twitterers known to be good negotiators to keep an eye peeled while he bargains in a showroom. He sends messages about how he's doing and they respond with advice.

There is now so much pressure on dealers that some of them routinely reveal their exact markup to the customer. The biggest dealer chain, AutoNation, has a website enabling customers to check inventories, list prices, and trade-in quotes for their ZIP code or anyplace else. Nobody dreamed that the customer would have those tools and more at hand when he walked into a showroom.

All that's nice but it's hindsight. Back then we didn't think it was easy, that someone had handed us a good living on a platter. One miscue could send a prospect to General Motors or to another Ford agency. We had to size up the customers quickly and accurately, we had to make a winning first impression, and we had to use our negotiating skills to keep the customers on track until we got their signatures on the sales forms. I didn't doubt that I could do all of it, and my self-confidence contributed mightily to my success.

The first day I was on duty I walked out to the sales floor in one of my two brand new suits. I was proud to see my name on the chalk board, showing that I was "up" that day. That's one thing that hasn't changed in the car business, the sales people who are on duty on any given day have "ups," taking turns greeting the customers as they walk through the door. A customer, too, is called an "up." You take the "up" who walks in when it's your turn.

My first "up" was a young guy. He saw a 1956 bright red Thunderbird convertible parked on the showroom floor. The T-bird we're talking about here is the original design, a two-seater with a powerful engine. Ford unveiled it late in 1954 as a 1955 model, rsponding to Chevy's Corvette, first rolled out in 1953. The Corvette was also a two seater, with a low-slung, fiberglass body. It had the wraparound windshield and swooping, slightly bulbous lines of all the GM products of that time. It looked sporty but it came with the old Chevy "stovebolt" six and a sluggish two speed automatic transmission.

Contrast that with the T-bird, also low-slung on a short wheelbase, but a trimmer, slimmer looking car with a bomb under the hood. Its 215 horsepower V-8 could run rings around the original Corvette. Some called it a banker's hot rod.

So the car was a stunner. The young guy walked over to it and asked me, "How big is the motor in this car?" Now you have to know that all the other salesmen, older fellows who were dubious about me, were eavesdropping on my talk with the young guy.

"How big is the motor in this car?" he asked

"Well," I said, gesturing with my hands, "that one is about four feet long and two feet high."

All the other salesmen were shaking their heads and wringing their hands.

"You're single, right," I asked the young guy.

"Yes."

"You can get a lot of women with this car."

Now the nuts-and-bolts type salesmen are sure that this is a sale down the drain. They're thinking that we're gonna be sued. They know men, even young guys, won't buy a car from a wiseacre like Gayle. But I went on.

"This car goes really fast. Don't worry about the motor yet. We've got a T-bird parked outside. Let's go for a ride."

The first goal was to get them into the demonstrator.

"Come on, let's go," I said in a tone that wouldn't take no for an answer.

We got into that beautiful car and drove down one of Burien's main drags, Ambaum Boulevard, to a bar that most of my co-workers went after work. They went there to drink a little and relax, but also to check out the girls who frequented the bar. We found a parking place right in front.

"Let's have a smoke and watch the attention you get," I said.

Sure enough, within two or three minutes after we lit our cigarettes a couple of real pretty girls got off work and came by, admiring the car. The young guy was startled, he'd never seen anything like it.

"Have you seen the new Thunderbird yet," I asked the girls.

"No," they said.

"Come here and have a look, it's nice," I told them.

They were impressed and the four of us stood around talking about the car for a while.

On the way back to the dealership I filled the young guy in on all the mechanical details. I explained to him that if he were buying the car on time (and how else would a young guy buy it?) for only a few dollars more a month he could have that optional 215 horsepower V-8. I told him about the advanced carburetion, the brakes, the suspension, the generous interior room for a two-seater, and so on. I did know all that stuff. I sold the car.

The important lesson I learned right at the beginning was to get at the purchaser's end result, the WIIFM, the "What's In It For Me." In the case of the young guy, it was to meet and date girls his age. I showed him how the Thunderbird would polish his image and help him get the girls. If he has that car now, he's still getting attention from the ladies because it has become a classic and even more admired than when it was new.

My turn came up the next day when an older couple walked in. They were walking around a four-door sedan. The 1956 Fords had a rakish body that also looked comfortable so I knew that they probably were already sold on comfort and style. Sure enough, the man began asking about motors.

"Oh we have three kinds," I said, "a yellow one, a blue one, and a red one. The red one goes the fastest. That's why it's important for your family's safety."

I knew from my uncle's excellent morning sales seminars that you didn't sell speed thrills to older people, they'd had enough of those.

So I linked speed to security and safety.

"When you step down on the gas with the red motor, it will whisk you around a truck on a hill safely and with room to spare."

"Do you have grandchildren?"

"Yes."

"Do they ride with you sometimes?"

"Yes."

There was my clincher, because Ford had just installed safety door locks that kids couldn't open and that held the doors closed much better in a crash.

"Well," I said, "you're going to be very happy with this car, it has the convenience of a four-door and the safety of a two-door because Ford just came out with these safety door locks. Get in the back seat and let me work them for you."

So they did. Then we took a demonstration ride. I sold that car.

I sold my third "up." Sold my first three "ups," much to the delight of my uncle but to the dismay of the other sales people, because I wasn't doing things in the conventional way. I'm not going to tell you that I sold every customer any more than I'll tell about standing barefoot in the snow selling magazines. I did well enough to be the number one salesman in the company for several years.

I learned what people really buy. I learned that the secret of sales success is to find out early on through questioning or shrewd guessing what the customer is actually after. I learned to paint a word picture of the end result, "you can get the girls with this car," or "your grandkids won't fall out of this car," then put the customer in the picture by showing him how the girls respond or how the door locks work. From the get-go, my sales experience was challenging, exciting, and financially rewarding.

• • •

My next job was not so successful but I'll tell you about it without any glossing over because in sales as in other areas of life we should learn from our mistakes. My mistakes taught me how to respond to people better when in later life I headed up sales teams.

To get on with the story, my uncle in Burien took an opportunity to invest in a going concern, a Ford dealership in Salem, Oregon. The Oregon dealership had been in the same family for years, the family had built it up, and it was well respected. My uncle asked me to go down to Salem to be the assistant sales manager and naturally

I couldn't say no to the man who'd given me my first break in sales. Then my uncle had a heart attack, went to the hospital, and made me general manager.

Sure I knew something about selling, but I knew next to nothing about managing and certainly very little about the other departments of a dealership, except for parts. All I knew about the service department came from taking cars there to have them repaired or maintained, and from working under the same roof with it. I knew it was an essential part of the business, but beyond that, not much.

The boys in the Salem shop probably would tell you that I knew less than zero about the service department. What I did know for certain was that we inherited most of the people from the previous owners of the dealership. They were old-timers, many of them, and had helped to make the business a success. That included the folks in the service department.

I'll never forget the head of the service department. Charlie was his name, a burly, outdoorsy type who'd been getting the job done for thirty years. Thirty years! One day I had some question about what was going on in the service department. I looked for him and he wasn't there.

"Oh, Charlie's out hunting," the assistant service manager said.

"What do you mean, out hunting," I asked.

"Every year when deer hunting begins, Charlie goes hunting."

Now I didn't like being left out of the loop, not knowing where the head people were. I was their boss after all. Of course had I stopped to think about it I would have realized that Charlie had been there longer than I'd been alive. This was his arrangement with the previous owners and he didn't have to clear it with anybody.

Instead of thinking I got upset and shot off my mouth. I raised my voice so that everyone in the shop could hear.

"You never told me anything about it. He didn't say anything about it. You tell him when he comes back to come to my office immediately."

A week later I went out to the service department. Charlie was there, just back from deer season, putting on his shop coat. The assistant shop manager, the accountant, and four or five mechanics were on the shop floor. In front of them, I let Charlie have it.

"How could you leave your job without telling me? How could you do such a stupid thing?"

"I've been doing this for thirty years. I go out hunting the first week of deer season. I always go."

His retort made me madder.

"That may be," I practically shouted, "but you don't take off without telling me. *Never* do that again!"

I'd really told Charlie off, hadn't I? Three weeks later I go out to the shop looking for Charlie and he's not there. This time it's elk season and Charlie's off, hunting elk. Did he tell me? Nope. I blew up.

"I told him not to go! He's fired! You have him come see me!"

In my defense, Charlie should have realized that there was a new ownership, that he might regard me as a punk kid in a temporary job, but that I was his boss for better or worse. He should have cleared his elk hunting with me. Still, I shouldn't have hit the ceiling, dressed him down in front of his subordinates, or told others that he was fired without telling him first.

None of what Charlie might have done or should have done cooled my righteous wrath. A week later I went out to the shop and there's Charlie, putting on his shop coat again, as if nothing happened.

"Charlie, what are you doing?"

"I'm going to work."

"I told you last time, the next time you do a thing like that without telling me, you're fired!"

My outburst and my raised voice brought everybody to a semicircle around Charlie, waiting to see what cantankerous old Charlie would do. Charlie pulled off his shop coat and threw it on the floor.

"Well I'll be damned! If I had known this job wasn't going to be permanent when I took it, I never would have took it in the first place!"

Later I found out that I'd handled Charlie in the wrong way.

My job ended soon after, and it was probably just as well. My uncle's health problems forced him to sell the dealership. I didn't want to stay in Salem, a nice, tidy town but one too small for my ambitions. Besides, my chances of staying on with a new ownership were slim to none. So I returned to Seattle and went back to selling cars.

• • •

Now, what had I learned about selling? I learned that, of course, you have to know the product, whether it's a car, an automatic car wash, a video game, or a house. But telling the customer about the virtues of the product is not going to make you a master of selling. It's finding out what the customer wants the product to do for him or her, then shaping your sales talk around the customer's wishes that makes sales.

Chapter Four

Lemonade from Lemons and a Way to Successful Selling

When I returned from Salem to Seattle I made lots of lemonade out of a really large lemon. In fact, I wound up making the biggest sale of my car selling career. Here's how it happened. I went back to work at my uncle's Ford dealership in Burien, this time as fleet sales manager. I was doing well, had a brand-new demonstrator to drive, and went one night to downtown Seattle for dinner and drinks. I'd had a little too much of both and fell asleep at the wheel just after crossing the Burien city limits.

I woke up soon enough. You could say that I awakened with a bang. That loud noise was the front end of my car hitting the rear end of the car in front. It jolted me out of my slumber. The driver of the car ahead was doing the right thing, waiting at a red light. The collision propelled the car ahead clear across the intersection and caved in the back of that car. My new demonstrator wasn't in such great shape either. The impact smacked the bumper, grill, front sheet metal generally, and tore open the radiator. Water was running all over the intersection.

I got out of my car and hurried over to the car I'd hit. By the time I got there, a great big guy was standing outside the driver's door, talking on a microphone. Practically speaking, in those days only law enforcement had microphone setups like that. A woman in the back seat was holding her neck and moaning, "Oh, I'm hurt."

"Are you the police," I asked the big guy.

"Yes, as a matter of fact I'm the chief."

He was actually the sheriff of the whole darn county, King County, and he was telling his troops he'd been in a wreck. Within a few minutes the squad cars were coming in from everywhere, red lights flashing and sirens blaring. I'd struck their leader. Things did not look good.

While the deputies were arriving and looking over the scene, the sheriff, Murray Gamrath, and I were talking. He looked down at the dealer plates and the plate surround on my bashed-in demonstrator.

"You work for Gene Wagner?" he asked.

I told him I did. With that, the complexion of things began to change. My uncle had been an active contributor and fund raiser for Murray's election.

"Let's take both cars to the dealership and have them repaired," I suggested.

Which we did. That cleared matters a bit but I was still worried about filing an accident report. I called a friend in the sheriff's department.

"How much trouble am I in? Can you go over and find out what's going on?"

"I'll call you back," he promised.

"Good news," he declared when he called back. "Murray already filed an accident report. He said that a third car cut in front of him, and cut him off while they were traveling toward the red light. He had to put on his brakes, leaving no time for the car behind (mine) to stop. The third car ran the red light and disappeared."

Of course it was all nonsense. Even if any of it were true, I should have gotten a ticket for following too closely or some such offense. But who was going to argue with the sheriff? What a relief!

"What kind of whiskey does Murray drink," I asked.

"He likes Scotch," my friend replied, naming the brand. I'd already learned that we lived about three blocks from each other.

I bought a bottle of Scotch, called Murray, and arranged to meet him at his house.

"We're neighbors," I said as I walked through Murray's door with the bottle of Scotch.

He and I proceeded to drink that bottle of Scotch and had a fine time doing it. That was the beginning of a good friendship. We socialized a fair amount. Murray introduced me to some people he knew in the state patrol and through them I was able to sell some patrol cars.

Indeed the whole episode worked out very well, except where the insurance company was concerned. The woman in the back seat of Murray's car was his mother-in-law. She spent a year going to downtown Seattle every week for treatments on her sprained neck, at the insurance company's expense.

But I'm yet to get to the big sale. One day Murray was having a party and invited me.

"I have someone coming over and I'd like you to meet him if you haven't."

The guest was Albert D. Rosellini, the governor of Washington state. He'd been in law and politics for a long time, and knew just about everybody.

"You know Al, don't you," Murray asked.

"No, I haven't had the pleasure," I replied.

Rossellini found out what I did and introduced me to one of the big wheels at Boeing aircraft, who was also at the party. "Oh, we're just putting out some bids for some cars," the Boeing guy told me.

I checked it out. "Some cars" was 500 cars! Did I ever get busy on that one.

I landed the contract and I'll tell you how I helped myself get it. I knew we would have some stiff competition from Chevrolet and, back then, Plymouth. So I met the purchasing people at Boeing and took them to dinner a few times. That didn't hurt. Knowing Rossellini didn't hurt.

Naturally we discussed business in an above-board way. The purchasing people dropped a few hints about the features or extras they wanted on their cars, so I had all the options covered in my bid. Service was important. I convinced them that we were close enough to handle that, and that we were capable of buying and doing the make-ready on all those cars. Naturally, price was the first consideration, but my extra knowledge was important, too. The *Ford Times* carried an article on the sale and it sure was a big deal for me. Soon after I'd won the bid Murray and I were having lunch, celebrating the delivery of those cars.

"Murray, our wreck was kind of a funny way to meet a guy, but I sure have enjoyed our acquaintance."

"Yeah, I can see why."

Lots of lemonade came from that big lemon.

• • •

After the big sale, I moved on to working with Success Motivation Institute, a transforming, life-changing event for me. Before we get into that, however, let me tell you where the rest of this chapter is going. First I want to explain what SMI was doing and how I became involved with it. Next we'll look briefly at three books that influenced me. All three have important messages, but it was the SMI training that opened my mind to them. Then I'll describe how my SMI program worked and how it led me to join forces with a truly remarkable man, Eric Berne, the author of *Games People Play.*

This is me in my salad days, when I was selling Fords and doing motivational speaking for Success Motivation Institute. From Salsesman's Opportunity magazine, vol. 84 (March 1964).

Paul J. Meyer, an authentic genius, founded SMI in 1960. At the time I'd never heard of Paul Meyer and certainly not of SMI. I was still in the car business, but was reading motivational books and sales books, as they were a dime a dozen. They were a mix of realistic instruction and some notions that were pure pie-in-the-sky, such as visualization unaccompanied by a plan for getting whatever was being visualized.

Still, I was intrigued and beginning to think in terms beyond the Ford dealership. A friend who was on the same wavelength told me, "I went to a meeting the other night, run by a representative of Success Motivation Institute. I think you'd be interested in that. It sounds like it's right up your alley." So I called the head office in Waco and I was lucky enough to talk to Paul Meyer himself. He encouraged me to come on down. I took a leave of absence, got on an airplane, went to Texas, and signed up for the program.

Paul and others had worked out the basic motivational program and developed successful sales methods. SMI was then connected with Baylor University in Waco. It's still in Waco and may still rely on Baylor people for some courses. It is now called Success Motivation International. Paul has more than 50 million copies of his work in print worldwide. Fifty million!

While at SMI and Baylor I took courses loosely grouped around the subjects of psychology, motivation, and public speaking. Then I became a divisional manager in Seattle, responsible for getting the SMI materials out to the public through sales talks and motivational speaking, I took on Uncle Gene as a partner. Later he went on to write books on leadership training and sales psychology.

Back then the materials consisted of a study manual, workbooks for the student to chart his or her progress in improving areas of his or her life, and spoken motivational books on those large 33 1/3 vinyl records, some read by the authors themselves. There were wire recorders and tape recorders then but they were big and boxy, clumsier to handle than a small record player. Paul had the right idea, using the most current technology of the time and using records that the student could repeat over and over again.

The repetition was much more effective than trying to cram everything into somebody's head in one sitting. After all, the Grand Canyon wasn't made in a single stroke. The Colorado River ran down there for hundreds of years, carving out the canyon. That was Paul's idea, take things slowly with lots of repetition. Dr. Cliff Williams of the Baylor psychology department did a whole album on parts of his lectures. One of the first records was from Napoleon Hill's *Think and Grow Rich*. Of course the technology changed over time, to a small player that you could carry in your car with you, then to various types of small tape recorders, and it's probably on IPod now.

Hearing parts of Dale Carnegie's *How to Win Friends and Influence People* inspired me to read the book. After I'd read it I wished that I'd read it before dressing down old Charlie, the service department manager back in Salem, Oregon. I should have talked to Charlie privately, in a friendly way, listened to his history with the company, told him that I didn't object to his hunting trips but that I needed to know where the important people in the dealership were each day. Would he please do me the small, easy favor of letting me know when he, such a significant man in the business, would be hunting? Probably that would have worked and kept Charlie on the job. There is, by the way, much more in Carnegie's book. If you haven't read it, I urge you to. The latest edition is still in print.

The next book I read was Hill's *Think and Grow Rich.* Hill lays out a program for tapping into the powerful forces of suggestion, psychic affinity, imagination and visualization to make money in a moral way. It, too, is still around. Please read it. The third book is Dave Johnson's *The Power of Positive Intimidation in Selling.* I'm not sure that "intimidation" really conveys what Johnson is driving at, but "positive" surely does. Johnson stresses the role of affirmation and avoiding those everyday negatives in sales and in life. It's no longer in print but you will find used copies on sale and in any good sized library.

I can't do justice to these books with these little summaries. Even if you're not in sales, you *are* in life, and the principles developed in these books will help you live more enjoyably.

After finishing my SMI work, I returned to Seattle from Waco and built up a very good business. Here's how I did it. I began by selling myself and the SMI program to our initial targets, car dealerships, real estate companies, in fact any sales company. I soon developed a "time sell" based on the principle that it takes the same amount of time to sell ten people as it does one. That meant group sales. So I'd focus on the owner of, say, a real estate company. I'd make an appointment with the boss.

"You certainly would agree that if you had people who'd invest in themselves, better themselves, and because of that, sell more, it would be good for the company and your bottom line," I'd ask.

"Yes," he'd reply. Of course he would.

"Well, if you already had these men or women who were interested in improving themselves and bettering your business, those are the kind of people you'd like to develop, isn't that right?"

"Yes." Who could say no to that?

"So, knowing that you've selected your people carefully, here's what I'd suggest. Let's have a breakfast meeting and if your guys step up to the plate, and are willing to invest in the SMI program, those are the guys you'd like to have, right?"

"Oh, yes, sure," he'd respond.

"Now then," I'd say, "given the great advantage to you and your business, what would you be willing to do to participate in this? Most people like to be met half way, I know I do, don't you?"

"Yes, that's right," he'd say.

At that moment it hit him, *wham!* He'd just agreed to pay half the cost of the SMI program! In case he didn't get it, I'd say, "Thank you for encouraging your best people by meeting them halfway and paying half of the program cost!"

Does that mean it was all smooth sailing? Not on your life. My first breakfast meeting was a disaster. Naturally, I was paying for the breakfast and the private dining room at a nice motel, because nobody is going to pony up the price of a meal to hear a sales presentation that they might reject. Besides, a free breakfast with a person's co-workers usually is a good draw. This was a real estate company. There were maybe twenty people in the room and since the SMI material was fairly pricey I was amusing myself by calculating how much I'd make over costs if I could sell even half of them.

The company president was there. He got up to introduce me, and said,

"I've got this guy here who is going to tell you about something."

Then he sat down. I was stunned. I had to introduce myself, state my qualifications, explain everything about the program, that they would only pay half for it, and so on, but nothing worked. They looked at their president, saw that he wasn't interested in anything but a free breakfast, and refused to buy.

I learned from that. The next time I wrote out on a card what I wanted the president to say, and made certain that he agreed to say it. I worked in a little byplay between us. After I made my

In this stunt I climbed a ladder to make a sale to a potential customer. From Salesman's Opportunity vol. 84 (November 1964)

presentation he knew I'd turn to him and say,

"Here's Mr. So-and-so, your wonderful president, he's so fabulous that he will pay half the cost for anybody who's interested. He really wants you to better yourselves!"

Then I said, "You're going to say *yes*!"

That made it work. That moved everybody to the closing, to the sale. I thought of other ways to move everyone along. In the case of large companies, I'd agree to variations on the amount that the company paid. In other situations, sometimes I'd stipulate that a certain percent of the folks at the breakfast meeting had to sign up before the president paid half. But I got so good at closing that I rarely had to absorb any of the materials costs myself.

At the time I had an accountant, Mike Thompson. Mike had a subtle sense of humor, which many accountants don't have, but if you are an accountant reading this, I'm sure that you have a good sense of humor, too. Mike came to my office and went over the numbers, and asked, "How is the group selling going?"

"It's going pretty well. The last three I sold *one hundred percent!*"

"A hundred percent? That's not very good."

This was obviously some sort of gag so I played along.

"I've heard of the accountant mentality, how you guys do strange things with figures that nobody else can understand. What do you mean?"

"It's a good program, isn't it? They'll do better if they buy it, won't they?"

"Yes."

"Well if it's so good and they're supposed to be so improved, you come brag to me when you get everybody so excited that some of them buy two!"

Nobody bought two, but enough of my listeners recommended me that I did a lot of motivational speaking. Recall that I was called among other positive things, a "walking enthusiasm generator." I spoke to the Los Angeles Chamber of Commerce, and delivered the keynote address at an annual meeting of the Junior Chamber of Commerce in New York. I was doing motivational speaking all around the country. In 1968 I was speaking at the San Fernando Lodge to the chamber of commerce or economic development group for the San Fernando Valley. That's how I met Eric Berne.

• • •

Eric was an original. He was an M.D. who also studied psychoanalysis. From his studies he developed the concept of transactional analysis, the idea that every meeting between two or more people is a type of transaction. He analyzed these transactions in terms of the three roles that could be assumed by each player, Parent, Adult, and Child. The Child could be willful, demanding, and unruly, the Adult, mature and calm, and the Parent, scolding or otherwise disciplining the Child. Grownups communicate best as Adults, but things don't always work out that way, as you'll see.

Eric saw patterns in the way different people in various settings respond to their "transactional" situations. He described these patterns as games, and gave them cute names, such as "Now I've Got You, You Son of a Bitch," or "See What You Made Me Do." In *Games People Play*, published in 1964, he popularized his ideas, although he never intended the book to appeal to the masses. It just did. It was a breakthrough volume with a catchy title, a book for the times, an instant hit, and up to now has sold maybe 6,000,000 copies. For a long while it was required reading in university courses in psychology and psychiatry.

Ironically, Eric's book got a big boost with the publication of Tom Harris' *I'm OK – You're OK* in 1967. Harris, like Eric, was an M.D. He joined Eric's transactional analysis group, becoming one of Eric's most devoted disciples. Harris' book displayed the Parent, Adult, and Child circles (of which more in a moment) on the cover of its first edition. In that and other ways he exploited the popularity of Eric's book while repeating and extending its themes.

Best of all for Harris' book, it was pitched to a popular audience, which Eric's wasn't. For that reason it outsold *Games People Play*, selling possibly 15,000,000 copies. What's important here is that it didn't overshadow Eric's book as much as it reinforced Eric's message and encouraged people to read and hear Eric. Eric was, after all, the original guru of transactional analysis.

Eric was a workaholic who'd much rather write than speak.

Despite that he was in tremendous demand as a speaker. He carried it off all right, but he was better in small groups, or his large therapy groups, or one-on-one. Speaking to chambers of commerce and company managers just wasn't his thing. He didn't like dressing up to those occasions because he couldn't wear the outrageously mismatched clothes he sometimes did, just for fun.

Anyway, we were both doing our gigs at the San Fernando Lodge, a huge building with several large, separate lecture halls. Eric had finished his talk and walked by my hall. Probably I drew him in because I was doing my thing, shouting, jumping up and down, getting the audience members so worked up that they'd shout and jump, too. He sat on the back row and watched. After I'd finished, he came up and introduced himself.

"I like what you do," he said. "I'd like to talk to you about doing seminars together."

As we were leaving we ran into Bobby Kennedy, who I'd seen earlier in the day. Eric had met Kennedy somewhere before and introduced me. I'd heard him described as little, but he was surprisingly tall. We exchanged a few pleasantries and moved on. I remember that meeting so well because not long afterward Kennedy was shot and killed.

Eric had diagrammed his Parent, Adult, and Child as circles labeled Parent on top, Adult in the middle, and Child on the bottom. He suggested the types of interaction that could happen with a diagram of two parallel Parent, Adult, and Child circles, each top to bottom. He drew lines between the two sets of circles to suggest how the interaction could develop. I set up the diagram on a big easel on the stage and drew lines with a heavy felt marker to show what could be happening. Now this was in 1968 or 1969, four or five years after *Games People Play* appeared. In the meanwhile his readers had suggested other games to Eric, and he had thought of some more himself.

One that I liked was "Divorce Court." One Adult would be a man in the bedroom looking for his cufflinks.

"Have you seen my cufflinks?" he asks his wife.

His Adult asks her Adult, which is the way we should communicate. Unfortunately, he "hooked" to another part of her personality, for whatever reason, as we didn't go into that in depth. He "hooked" as Eric liked to say, to her Parent. And I'd draw a line from his Adult up to her Parent. Her Parent "hooked" to his Child, and said,

"I don't know where your cufflinks are! Why can't you take care of them yourself? Take care of your own things!"

Now if he is successful he will respond, not as a Child, but as an Adult, trying to "hook" to her Adult.

"I don't know, honey, I just though you maybe saw them lying around," he'd say. And I'd draw a line straight across from Adult to Adult. But his Child might take over.

"One of the reasons I married you was to take care of me," he'd shout. "I don't know why you can't look after my things, to hell with the damn cufflinks, I'm going to work anyway!"

He jumps in the car and burns the tires all the way down the road, to a big game called "Divorce Court."

Because Eric didn't write the book for lay people, you might say that I was the popularizer of it.

Eric and I traveled all over the country, even to Hawaii. We worked with real estate boards, chambers of commerce, and various companies, including the management of the *Wall Street Journal*. Our technique was to ask the management of an interested company to describe the games that people were playing in their offices. Then we would work those games into our presentation. Eric would usually be there to answer questions and sign copies of his book.

If we made a long-term commitment I'd hold workshops, as I did with the *Wall Street Journal*, and Eric would go back to his writing, his hospital work, and his private psychiatric practices, one in San Francisco, the other in Carmel. Otherwise, I'd make the presentation and Eric would be there to chat and sign his book afterwards. Then we'd move on to our next gig.

Eric was a fascinating guy. Once he picked me up at the San Francisco airport and drove me to his house in his Maserati. It was the first Maserati I'd been in. He acted like he was a terrible driver. The car roared all the way because he pretended that he didn't know how to shift out of first gear. You can imagine the racket we made as we zoomed up and down San Francisco's hills in first gear in that flashy, powerful car.

"What are you doing with a car like this," I asked.

He laughed.

"Well," he said, "my Child said 'I want it;' my Adult said, 'You can afford it,' and my Parent said, 'Drive carefully.'"

Later I found out that he knew how to operate a manual shift. His ride through San Francisco in low gear was just one of his wacky stunts.

Eric had a beautiful house. The living room was bare except for a set of drums. When he wanted to relax or relieve his frustrations, he'd play the drums.

"This is where I let my Child out," he'd say.

Some people criticized Eric for having a smarty, smart-alecky humor. I didn't see that. I thought that he had the wry, self-depreciating sense of humor of a man who could laugh at himself.

Eric wrote a lot. *Games People Play* was only one of his many successful books. He took his writing seriously, at least while he was at it. This was back in the typewriter days. He'd throw a fresh page in the typewriter, run it through, throw in another, and so on. At the end of a writing session he'd count the pages. Sometimes when his writing wasn't going well he'd wad up the pages and throw them into the corner.

"At least I got two-three pages out of all that," he'd remark.

He solved his writing problem when IBM came out with its first electric wide carriage machine. He bought one, then bought a roll of newsprint. He figured out how to hang the newsprint from a wall and feed it into the typewriter.

"How are you doing with the book?" someone would ask.

"Great!" he'd say. "Last night I did three yards!"

What a character!

It wasn't long after our association ended that he died. He had a heart attack, brought on by his maniacal work schedule and his failure to take proper care of himself despite his M.D. He went into the hospital and it looked like he would pull through. In fact he was sitting up in bed reading the proofs of his *What Do You Say After You Say Hello?* He suffered a massive heart attack and died.

That was in July 1970. He was only sixty.

• • •

Meanwhile I was doing my Success Motivation Institute seminars and decided to offer a series on real estate sales combining what I'd learned from my work with Eric, my SMI studies and presentations, and what I'd picked up along the way about selling real estate. I called the seminar "Pacific West's Series on Real Estate Fundamentals." At the time I'd never sold a square inch of real estate, so I had experts in real estate law and in mortgages talk to my groups. Otherwise I handled things myself. Looking back, I'd say that I was pretty young and nervy, but it worked. I've saved one of my brochures from those days, presenting a four-step sales program beginning with a session on Games People Play. It was a good opener because everybody knew that book, even if what they knew about it was half baked or wrong.

One of the things I did was illustrate the need for honesty with a chicken story. It seems that this butcher had enjoyed a busy day and had only one plucked chicken left. It was a scrawny thing, hanging up by his counter. A woman, one of his best customers, walked into his shop and asked for a chicken. He showed her the one he had left, which he admitted wasn't so great. But then he had an inspiration.

"Wait," he said, "I have another one under the counter."

He took the scrawny chicken in his right hand, slid it under the counter where she couldn't see it, passed it to his left hand, then held it up in his left hand for her to see. Of course it was the same chicken.

"This one's a little better, don't you think," he lied. "Which one do you want?"

She thought for a moment, then said, "I'll take them both!"

That story got some appreciative laughs, and softened them up for the important presentation.

Then I'd move on to the "gate selling" method, illustrating it by drawing an arrow on the left, followed by three oblong rectangles on the right. The arrow represented getting the client's

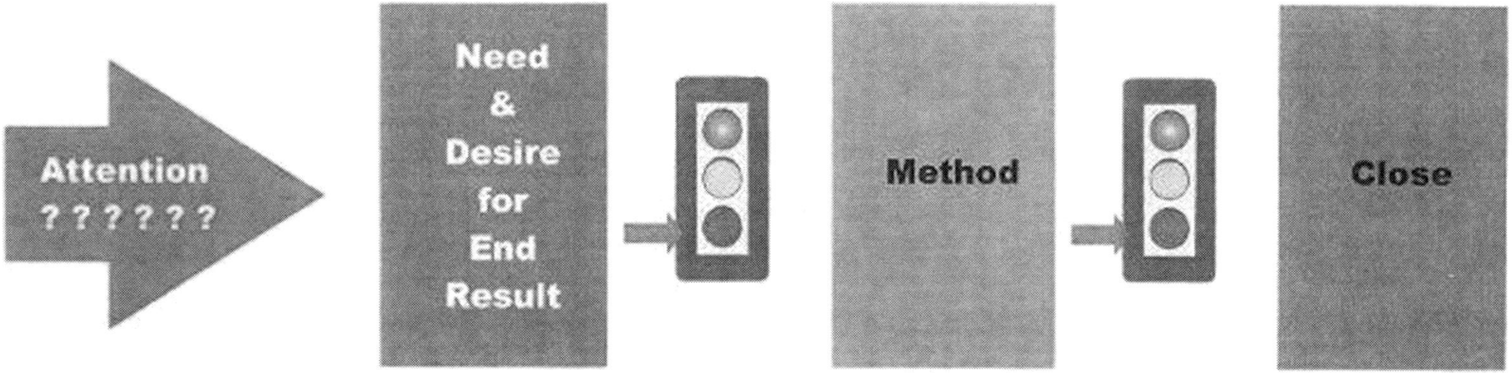

My refinement of the 'gate selling" method, explained in Chapters Four and Five. Gate selling envisioned moving through gates from one phase of the sale to another but I believe that the seller's visualizing green traffic lights is more effective. Sukey Janes diagram

attention. The first rectangle stood for establishing the client's need or desire for the house and lot, or whatever they were selling. The next rectangle involved the method used to make the sale, based on their understanding of the client's need or desire. The third rectangle was the closing, actually finishing up the sale.

I emphasized that if they didn't close, no matter how great the rest of it was, they'd wasted their time and money. Sometimes a successful close involves overcoming stalls and objections that crop up at the last moment, so I devoted a lot of time to dealing with stalls and objections.

I told them, too, that before they moved from identifying need or desire to a sales method, or before moving from a sales method to the close, they had to wrap up each phase as they went along. The "gate selling" method suggested a gate opening between each of the phases, or rectangles, but I didn't like the gate metaphor. It wasn't dramatic enough. Instead I told them that they had to have a green light. I drew traffic signals between the need and desire rectangle and the method rectangle, and the method rectangle and the close rectangle. I told them to make sure that they were visualizing a green light before they moved on to the next step.

Had they, for example, demonstrated an understanding of the property and merged that understanding with the client's needs or desires? Had they employed a sales method leading to a smooth closing, when they get the client's signature on the contract? Had they answered all questions fully? Had they dealt with objections? Had they tidied up everything, left no loose ends, so they could move on to the closing?

Back to the arrow. I said that the way to get the client's attention was to get him off what he was thinking about and on to what you, the seller, want him to think about. You do that by asking him questions about himself and his reason for getting in touch with you. He has to answer the questions and focus his attention on your concerns. Then you bring him around to what he needs or desires, the first rectangle.

I'd select somebody from the audience, say his name was Joe, who probably had no reason to buy anything in Acapulco. Through questions I'd get him around to admitting that he'd worked hard, needed a break, and convince him that we'd go to Acapulco to look at some property. I'd established in Joe a need or desire. I'd moved him from the first rectangle. I had him in the second, or method, rectangle. Now I had to use the proper method, or methods, to move him to the closing. So he packs his bags, in fantasyland, of course, since we're still in the seminar, and I show up at his door on a motorcycle during a pouring rain. And I'd say, "Hop on Joe, you and your bags and I are going to Acapulco on my motorcycle!"

Then I'd turn to Joe in the audience and ask him "What do you think of that?"

Joe would answer from the audience, "Hickok, you're insane! We can't go to Mexico on a motorcycle! And in the middle of a rainstorm! Get out of here!" So, my method was bad, I'd failed to move beyond the second rectangle. I had to begin all over again.

The second time I'd say, "Joe, I apologize for my stupidity, this time we have an airplane to take us to Acapulco."

"Great," he'd say, but when we climbed aboard I'd announce, "Joe, take the controls, you're flying us to Acapulco."

"Hickok, you're a fruitcake," Joe would shout from the audience. "I don't know anything about flying! You're crazy as a loon."

By this time the audience was giggling and really into it. Everyone realized that I was still stuck on that second rectangle, that I hadn't visualized the green light.

Finally I got Joe to Acapulco on a regular airline flight. But my work wasn't done. I'd have to finish with the second rectangle, to show him the property, show him a picture of how the property is superbly suited to him, and put him in the picture of the tropical paradise having everything within reach for a lot less money than he'd pay in the U.S. That time the sales method clicked. (Little did I know then that I'd someday be selling condos and timeshares in Acapulco.)

Now we're in the third rectangle, the closing. Here the buyer's stalls and objections would crop up, if they were going to, "I have to consult with my brother-in-law," or "I have to sleep on it," and so on. At last, objections overcome and stalls answered, we'd close.

• • •

In the next chapter I'll demonstrate how all this works in practical selling. For now, I'd like you to come along with me on a skiing trip to Lake Tahoe. It happened during one of my long periods of bachelorhood. Here I worked out a variant of the "gate selling" method that I call "Plan A – Plan B." I sure had a lot of fun doing it, as you'll see.

While I was waiting for a chair lift I saw this attractive young woman also waiting for a lift. The routine is for people who are by themselves to raise their ski poles and call out "single" to team up with other singles to fill up a chair. So I caught her eye, raised my pole, shouted "single, single," and steered her into the lift beside me.

I thought I'd try a little "gate selling" since she was strapped in and couldn't escape for a few minutes. So I said:

"What's your name?"

"What's your job?"

Where do you live?"

She was looking sideways at me, not making eye contact, obviously treating me as somebody she's only going to share a ride with. She answered my questions with, let's say, an evident lack of enthusiasm. But I kept at it.

"I see you're by yourself," I said, "or are you here with a girlfriend?"

"Yes, I'm here with a girlfriend, but I can't find her. She's lost."

"That's good," I said. "Did you come up here thinking you might meet some guys?"

"Oh, stop!"

"Why sure you did. I'm here with a friend of mine, but he's happily married so he won't be looking for a girl, but I'm a single guy."

"Oh."

After letting a little more time go by, I asked, "Did you know that most of us here, including us, are functioning under Plan A?"

"What's Plan A?" she asked.

This was the best possible way to wedge into someone's

thinking, to get them to stop thinking about what they're thinking about and to start thinking about what you want them to think about. Now she's tuned in, wanting to know what I want her to think about.

"What's Plan A?"

"Well, you're probably going to ski hard, maybe somewhere down a challenging hill. You'll stop for a breather and see a guy who really gets to you. You'll stop and you'll chat a bit, and maybe when skiing's through you'll go to the bar, one of those happy hour bars hereabouts. And," I concluded, "that's pretty much the standard deal, probably what you'll do, right?"

"Well, maybe."

I went on. "You're hoping to meet that guy or some other guy in the bar, maybe you'll have a few drinks. You've still got your ski outfit on, maybe you're a little tired, but you have a few more drinks, get a little tipsy, and then you say to the guy, 'Maybe we'll see you later at the disco.' And the guy will say, 'Yeah, maybe we'll see you.' So you exchange names and other pleasantries, and off you go. Then you go home, get dressed, go out, have a big dinner, drink some wine, and then head for the disco.

"By now you really are tired, a little sore, feeling a little logy, a little drunk. Then you run into the guy you've met, so you dance and drink some more. Maybe, if everything goes right and you and the guy have the right chemistry, you might get lucky and go to his hotel or your hotel. Or maybe you're both too exhausted to make anything happen. Isn't that about the way Plan A works? Wouldn't Plan B be better?"

Now she's not really sure what kind of pervert she's riding with, and we're almost at the place where we get off and change to another lift. But I've not done too badly. With the gate selling method I've gone some distance toward my goal. I have established the need and desire for after-hours partying. And I've cast doubt on the end result, some lively sex, by following Plan A. Well, at least I've wrapped up the first part. I guided my woman friend over the slippery spots to the next lift. And we're once more side by side in a chair. She still isn't sure about the loony tune she's riding with so I decide to do a take-away. I decide to say nothing about Plan B until she asks.

Finally she couldn't stand it any more.

"What's Plan B?" she almost shouted.

"Well, Plan B goes like this. Let's just say, for example, that you and I get along all right and we're both very good skiers, so we're going to go down the Black Diamond, one of the more challenging runs. We might fall down a couple of times. I help you up and you help me up and we'll roll in the snow and laugh a little, and stop and look at the view and ski all the way to the bottom, relaxed now and chatting some. We get on the chair, have two more runs, and a lot of fun.

"When we get down to the last run, instead of going into the bar, drinking a lot, going out to eat, going disco dancing, listening to all the lines and lies we're going to tell each other, and listen to all the lies that everyone around us is telling, instead of that we'll go right to my place. We'll have a nice shower, be refreshed, invigorated, and not be drunk. We'll jump into bed and have some great sex."

By this time her eyes are big as saucers. She's still thinking, "I'm stuck in this chair again with this nut." But I could tell that she was more interested in Plan B.

"When you stop to think about it," I went on, "Plan B makes sense, because, back at my place we've already had our good time, we've accomplished Plan A's end result at the beginning. Now we can get dressed and go out for a wonderful dinner. We have energy, we're sitting there having some wine, and you have those beautiful rosy cheeks. There's nothing prettier than a girl who's just made love. Here we are looking at the other people who are still on Plan A. They're just now having dinner; they're not even all the way drunk yet.

"Then we're going to go dancing. We'll look great on the dance floor. We've already been intimate, so everybody is going to be jealous of us for not wasting time on introductions because we've already been there; we're out dancing already, having fun. Hey, who knows, we might go back to my room and get lucky again."

By this time she's laughing, she's chuckling, and what's even more important, she's nodding her head, because all the way through my fantasy narrative I've interrupted to say, "Don't you see how this works? Wouldn't you agree that this makes sense?" So I'm getting lots of positive closes all along there.

Sure enough, after a few more runs down the hill, a few more jokes, a few more comments about Plan B, I tell her, "I just happen to have a nice cold bottle of champagne chilling in my room. No guarantees, no promises, but why don't we go back there and have a little start on the first part of Plan B, just to see how it goes? Nothing to lose."

"I don't know. I gotta find my girlfriend."

"Well, I gotta find my friend who I came here with."

We found them, explained the situation, they understood perfectly, and went their separate ways. I took the young woman back to my hotel, and true to the script, we had a wonderful time. In fact, we had such a wonderful time that I took the Plan A – Plan B selling routine to another ski resort.

At the second resort a young woman seemed to be playing along until we got to the end of the lift. Then she said, "See that big guy over there, he's my husband, waiting for me to get off the chair." I got out of there in a hurry, but most of the time Plan A – Plan B worked well.

To show you how gate selling works in the world of real estate, I'll fast forward to my recent sales in the Lomas del Centenario development.

Chapter Five

Practical Selling and Practical Self-Improvement

In this chapter I'll break into my chronological approach to tell you about "gate selling" in the here and now. Then I'll drop back into my life's time frame to tell you about getting out of motivational speaking. Despite my leaving motivational speaking, much of my SMI experience stayed with me. It's been incredibly valuable and I want to share that value with you.

Our Lomas del Centenario development began with advertising. We advertised in newspapers, magazines, and after the first few sales, by word of mouth. Several years ago we advertised in the Seattle Sunday paper during an especially gloomy, rainy Seattle winter and Seattle folks rang our phones all day. It was an extreme example of a *desire* for an alternative to overcast winter skies. Few had a *need* for a warm climate unless they were old and arthritic. And there are a lot of warm climates.

So I had to create a desire for *this* warm climate.

"What lifestyle is particularly pleasing to you?" I'd begin.

"Are you semi-retired and looking for a permanent place? Do you plan to escape the bad weather back home while you return to enjoy those northern Minnesota summers? Or, are you fully retired and looking for a permanent home in a warm climate?"

While asking these questions and others, I'd have my paper and pen out, taking notes. That activity helped my notoriously weak short-term memory, but that was not the only reason, because the clients got used to seeing me with pen and paper. When and if we got to the closing and I pulled out pen and paper again, they weren't startled by the idea that I was getting ready to ask them to sign a contract. They were used to pen and paper. More on that issue later.

From reading and experience I knew that the way to create a desire for *our* climate was not just to ask questions of my clients but to ask them in a relaxed, friendly atmosphere. We asked our clients to pay their airfare to La Paz but I always met them at the airport and took them to a nice hotel where the company paid for the first two nights. I took them to breakfast, then showed them the city of La Paz. The method here was to paint the picture of La Paz and put them in the picture. We drove by the beaches, the stores, the banks, went to a contemporary shopping mall with its huge supermarket and drove out the four-lane road to our development. They could see that this was a foreign country, all right, but not a hole-in-the-wall place where everyone was surviving by running some tourist racket.

I made it clear that La Paz was not "touristy" like some places in Mexico, that it was a real Mexican city. The culture was open, friendly, and warm, not centered on moneymaking or hustling tourists. I stressed the lower cost of living, the low rate of crime and drug use, the affordable, excellent medical care, the slower pace of life, the very low property taxes, and of course the wonderful climate. They'd already seen the shopping, tasted the excellent food, and sampled the entertainment. I explained that in Mexico you could own your own home through a bank trust, not like Hawaii or England, where noncitizens must lease.

The next picture to put them in was the development itself. I'd already driven them by and through some developments that were OK, but where the houses were a bit cramped or the lots a little small. Our lots were generous and the houses nicely sized. They were not too much for an older couple to maintain, especially not with the eager, hard-working, available, relatively low-wage help. I showed them the lots, views, and model homes.

All that time they were asking questions about La Paz, our residential development, the infrastructure, and whatnot. I made it a point to answer them fully. Meanwhile I was showing them around, saving what I thought was the best lot or house for them, based on our conversations. Now then, people don't like to make personal decisions, I don't care who they are. They may have a job that requires them to make decisions. That doesn't mean that they like making personal decisions.

"You have your choice of lots (or houses)," I'd say, "but based on what you've told me about yourselves, I'd choose this one." See, it's a choice, not a decision. Ninety-nine point nine percent of the time that was the one they'd buy.

Let's put all this another way. I began by gathering information, painting a picture for the clients based on that information, putting them in the picture, both the bigger picture in La Paz and the smaller one in our development. Did I begin by pulling out floor plans, estimating costs, describing construction, and estimating time from beginning to completion and other mundane stuff? You bet not. Instead I sold my clients on what the La Paz area would do for them, the WIIFM, the "What's In It For Me?"

Once I'd explained the WIIFM, we'd move on to floor plans, costs, and all the rest of it, as a sort of auxiliary to the main matter of living in the delightful La Paz area. After all that was taken care of, it looked like the light was green to that third rectangle. As we go to the closing, we have to keep in mind that people don't like to say no. It's the second thing that they don't like to do. So they stall, or they find something to object to.

We're really going toward the close from the beginning, when I'm asking about the goals and objectives. All through this we are talking about something they want, which is a better picture of their life. We aren't talking about something I want, for instance selling the biggest lot, or the best view, or the most extensive floor plan. All along I've been making statements that it's easy for them to agree with, such as "isn't the bay beautiful at this time of day," or "isn't this a nice view?" Of course they can say, "No, it stinks," but since people don't like to make decisions, they'd rather agree with statements as long as they weren't rushed or pushed by insulting or frightening words.

While establishing desires and working through the sales method I never mentioned the word "show." People don't like to be "shown," because it often means that you think they don't have the brainpower to understand something. They're smart enough to see it themselves. I never said, "do you get it?" or "do you follow me?" I'd say something like "the bank trust arrangement is an excellent program but the details are a little different than they might be in the U.S., so I'll share them with you and ask you to ask any questions afterward."

Notice the word "share." People like to have things "shared" more than they like to be "shown."

At the closing when I'd pull out the pen – remember the pen? – I'm not displaying something they haven't seen before. It's not like I'm unlimbering the artillery to fire at them with words like, "Let's sign the contract." Too often they balk, "*Sign*! I didn't say anything about *Sign*!" Or they think "*Contract*! Here I am in this strange country with a weird legal system and now they want a contract!"

Instead I'd say to a couple, "Here is the paperwork. Let's go over it and see how it looks. I'll answer any questions that you have." If it is OK, then I'd say, "Mary" (we'd been on a first name basis from the get-go when I said, "Hi, my name's Gayle. May I call you by your first names?") I'd say "Mary" because I knew that women made the final decision, "Mary, just put your name here, and, what's the date today?" No mention of "sign," no mention of "contract," it was "name" and "paperwork." By asking the date I was drawing them into the buying process, getting their participation. The last step was "John, if you'd just put your name here," then it's wrapped up and they've joined the family of proud and happy owners.

Sure, the ending wasn't always so easy. That's when the stalls and objections came in. Remember that people don't really like to say no, any more than they like to make decisions. They may say, "We don't have the down payment." Well, if that's really the problem, I should have learned that through my questions before then. My fault. But the best way is to answer a negative is with a question or a positive. Expressing absolute confidence in the customer's financial soundness is one way to be positive.

"I'm not prying into your financial affairs," I'd say, "but how long would it take for you to convert some assets to cash? We can postdate the paperwork and hold it until that time."

I'm telling them that I'm sure they have the money, and usually they'll work it out. But often the stall or objection really wasn't the problem. So I'd begin to go over everything again. These were the "tellmeisits."

"Tell me, is it me?"

"No, you're great!"

"Tell me, is it the weather?"

"No, the weather is terrific!"

I'd continue, until we get to the problem. Is it La Paz, is it the trust agreement, or is it the banking system?

If it's La Paz, I'd say, "I've lived near La Paz for years, and you'll find everything right here," and show them again if I had to. If it was the banking system, I'd tell them about my own bank account in La Paz. If they doubted the trust arrangement I'd explain that I was a lot owner too and that in my opinion the trust was perfectly fair and OK. Would I be a lot owner if I thought otherwise?

You wouldn't believe some of the stalls.

"I have to show it to my dog. If he barks twice it's a sale."

"I have to clear it with my brother Frank." That's a favorite, even though brother Frank's never been west of the Mississippi, lived in an apartment all his life, and knows nothing about real estate.

The best way to answer objections is to take the blame on yourself.

"If you have to put your dog or brother Frank to all that trouble, then there's something I haven't adequately explained." As soon as Mary and John see that I'm taking the blame on myself, they begin to sympathize with me, work with me to overcome the objection, and almost always move on to the close.

Sometimes a client will say, "Oh, gosh, my wife and I have talked it over and we're not going to buy anything but you are such a great guy, we want a stack of your business cards to hand out to our friends." Yeah, right! They're not going to buy anything from me but they're going to have their friends buy from me? Tell me another one. That trick is called "carding you off."

They think that "carding you off" is a compliment or that you'll take it as a compliment. It isn't of course. The only way to turn it around is to take it as a negative and convert it into a positive.

"I'm flattered that you want to have my cards. I will give you some. But first, I know that I failed to convince you that we have the best development in Mexico right here. Tell me how I've failed and what your objections are." If it was the dog and brother Frank, or if it turns out to be Mexican banks, then I know how to get the sale back on track.

Sometimes, though, an objection isn't really an objection or a stall. People really do want time to think it over.

"OK Mary and John," I'd say. "I do have other clients coming in, but I can meet you at the hotel at either 10:40 tomorrow morning or at 2:20 tomorrow afternoon. It's your choice."

Once again, they're choosing, not deciding, but they are pinned down to a specific time, not say 10 o'clock which can mean anything up to 10:30 for some people.

"I think that 10:40 would be best," Mary says. So we'd meet, and if I'd done my work well, they'd sign.

• • •

Sometimes I have to use a little ingenuity to close. My favorite spot for consummating deals is the Bay of Dreams down the coast from La Paz. It's a beautiful spot, with deep blue, sparkling water and a smooth, sandy beach. The first-rate restaurant is a much better place to close a deal than the office. I'm out there often, and so receive very good service. Whenever the paperwork comes out the staff knows I'm near a close and leaves me and my clients alone. Now this couple was very nice, very proper, and I suspected that they were deeply religious. We'd had a fun time, and I'd gotten everything but their "names" on the "paperwork."

"You know, we always pray about everything before we make a decision," Mary said as she turned to John.

I put down my pen.

"I can really understand and appreciate that, and you're very honest people. I agree with your idea. Let's pray about it together right now."

I got down on my knees and folded my hands on the tabletop. All the staff in the restaurant stopped whatever they were doing and stared at us, thinking, what's that crazy Hickok doing now? Mary and John hesitated.

"Come on, come on," I said. "Let's pray now. I'm inviting you to pray with me. Don't mind those other people, who cares who's looking at us, this is between us and God."

I put it this way: "Dear God, these people are looking for a place to retire, relax, and be comfortable. Please help me to explain to them something I may have left out because evidently I've made some mistakes here. Can you coach me a little bit?" After a pause I looked at Mary.

"Is there something special I forgot?"

She replied that she wanted some guidance from the Lord.

"I agree with you completely. Thanks, Lord. I hope that you sent us the right inspiration and do the right thing for these people. Now, Mary, just give me your name right here. I'm sure the Lord's approving of this. I got a really good message when we were down on our knees."

They bought.

Now, that may be a little bit of grandstanding or showmanship, but I was not trying to be slick. I've never tried to be tricky or to con people, because I hate con artists and tricky people. They give selling a bad name and hurt the business for the vast majority of us who are honest. I'm not Mr. Smoothtalker who tricks people into doing something they don't want. We'd already gone through all the things they wanted and needed. I just nudged them along a little bit, with an easy process that made it painless.

Why is the closing so important? Because if you don't close, you don't make the sale. That seems so obvious that it isn't worth saying. But that's where too many sales people are tripped up. They don't stumble over mountains, they stumble over molehills. A molehill is "I have to show this to my dog" or "I have to pray over this." When they hear that, sales people should at once take responsibility for the problem, and respond with "I appreciate your situation, I would do the same thing if I were in your position, and let's see where I've failed you." That gets the buyer on the side of the seller because the seller is the one at fault, who needs the buyer's help in straightening out the issue so they can move on to the close.

Instead of doing that, too many people in sales give one of three wrong responses. They say, "Oh, uh, gee, well, when and if your dog agrees to the sale, let me know, here's my card." Ninety percent of the time the seller never sees the potential buyer again. Or they reply with heavy pressure, like "Aren't you man enough to sign this right now," which is off-putting. Or they focus on themselves, not the buyer and the buyer's needs. They say something, however well they phrase it, that means "I've done my job, I've driven you all over town and the development, I've explained everything, and still you don't get it, you dumb jerk." That will kill a sale every time. So let's pay attention to the closing, because if we increase the percentage of closings by even a few points, more people will have their needs and desires met.

• • •

OK, we've jumped forward to how I used the "gate selling" method in the real world. The "gate selling" method was motivational, sure, but it was one-on-one or one-on-two. It was quiet, it was restrained, and it ended positively, usually with a sale. Now I'm going to tell you why I got out of motivational speaking. It was because, unlike selling, it was group work, was loud, was unrestrained, and was unending.

Here's how motivational speaking worked, usually. First I'd research the business, learning what they thought they needed to do, where they needed to go, and what they wanted. I'd learn some of their buzzwords. Then I'd go into the meeting, be introduced, run to the podium, and soon be shouting and waving my arms about their needs and wants, throwing in a few of their buzzwords. By that time the sparks were flying around the room, and the sales manager's grinning from ear to ear.

"We're going to have our best year ever," I'm shouting. "It'll be the most dynamic year of our life. YES, we're going to do this!"

Everybody's cheering and stomping their feet. Once in a while I'd become so carried away with my own rhetoric that I'd peel off my jacket, throw it in the corner, yank off my tie.

"You have a great sales manager," I'd shout. "He'd give you the shirt right off his back!" I'd rip off my shirt, with the buttons popping off and bouncing around the floor. And they'd be screaming and crying, with some of the men, at least, tugging at their own shirts. If I was selling SMI motivational materials, too, I sold a cartload.

But do you know? Soon those cheering and weeping folks would be the same people they were before. They'd get out of bed the next morning and get ready for the day with no more enthusiasm than they had before my seminar. They would go on working the way they always had. They might do the workbooks or listen to the tapes for a while, but would rarely stay with the program to the end. About one or two percent would complete the work or internalize my pep talk.

I became disillusioned with motivational speaking. It paid very well, but the "unending" part was that most of the people undergoing the motivational experience were not equipped with very good self-starters. They had to be revitalized regularly with follow-ups, and that wasn't practical, usually. Let me make it clear that there was nothing wrong with the SMI materials. The problem was with people's failure to profit from them. The situation was a lot like those evangelistic tent revival meetings. Folks in those meetings would be shouting and rolling around on the ground, confessing their sins, and all that. Then they'd go back to their old bad habits. They'd backslide.

• • •

Eventually I cut my ties to SMI but I owe a life changing experience to its founder, Paul J. Meyer. Some folks think that people like Paul never had a real job. They think these motivators cook up halfway phony stuff to try to get people to do what they can't do themselves. I assure you that wasn't the way with Paul.

Paul grew up in a family that was not poverty-stricken but certainly not well-to-do. His father was a craftsman who rarely praised anyone in his family but demanded self-reliance, hard work, and perfection from Paul. After graduating from high school in 1946 and completing his army service, Paul began selling life insurance. He had already successfully sold magazines, earned good money by contracting farm labor, and built himself into a magnificent physical specimen through weight lifting.

Paul's dynamism, hard work, bold approach to sales, and

incredible self-confidence made him a leader in life insurance sales when he was still in his early twenties. He had all the material trappings of success including, by age 27, a net worth of a million dollars. That was when a million dollars meant substantial wealth. By then he was in charge of sales for a rapidly expanding insurance company in Florida. Little did he know that the company president was stealing from his own firm. One night the president found it convenient to load up the company's belongings and decamp to Alabama, where the company was chartered. Paul learned the hard way about the phrase "fly-by-night."

Paul was not a company officer or board member, just the head of sales. He had no responsibility at all for the situation. Yet he stayed in Florida, personally carried the company's liabilities, and found other jobs for the members of the sales force he created. He wound up tens of thousands of dollars in debt, but by going back to work he cleared that debt quickly.

Finally Paul decided to help others achieve their life goals by founding Success Motivation Institute. When he went on the road to sell his own program he was a smashing success. Over the years he also sold houses, a farm, and condos. The man could sell anything. Paul once told me that I was the second best salesman he'd ever encountered. He never told me who was the best, but I suspect that Paul thought of himself as the best.

SMI taught a variety of motivation courses when I joined up, but the one that has stuck with me over the years is simple, direct, and needs no technology other than a pencil or pen and a pad of paper. No doubt SMI has modified and strengthened its programs over the years. If you are determined to improve all the areas of your life using the latest SMI thinking, go to the SMI (now Success Motivation International) website and begin there. Until you do, or if you want to try the simple stuff first, follow and apply my explanation. Believe me, it works!

• • •

The key to Paul Meyer's impact on me is his definition of success: the successful person is one who continually realizes, or advances toward, a predetermined goal or set of goals. Paul argued, and I believe he's right, that too many of us emphasize financial success, simply making lots of money. Paul makes more money in half a year than most people make in a lifetime, so someone could respond, "well, that's easy for him to say, he doesn't have any financial worries, so he can bother with all that other stuff." That response misses the point. Paul made his money at the same time that he moved toward predetermined goals in all areas of his life.

Let's take an example. After going bust and paying off his debts Paul wanted to get back into life insurance, this time by founding his own company. He raised the capital from friends who knew that he would focus all of his genius on making the company go. Then he discovered that he would have to pay a bribe to be chartered in the state he'd selected to do business in.

The bribe was dressed up as a "consultantship" but it was understood that the "consultant" would do no work and the whole thing was off the books. Paul could have paid the bribe but bribery violated his deeply held social and spiritual beliefs, and compromised the goals he had set for himself in those areas. He resolved never to be involved with life insurance again, returned the money his backers had advanced, and moved on to other activities that led eventually to his founding of SMI.

Paul's conviction that we spend too much time and energy on material success at the expense of other life goals wasn't new. It's in any good self-improvement manual or book on selling. Paul's breakthrough was to identify the six areas that we could improve: physical, mental, social, financial, spiritual, and familial or family life. A successful individual is one who blends all of them together to reach a predetermined life goal. Beyond identifying the six, what made Paul outstanding was his ability to excite people about writing down their goals. At the beginning of every year, using a separate page for each area of life, Paul emphasized "what the mind can conceive and believe, it can achieve." So put down your goal, no matter how wild it seems.

The next thing is to write down the obstacles and roadblocks to achieving the goal, at least as they appear to you at the outset. Now that those are down, what are the methods or projects for overcoming those obstacles? Write them down. Now comes the big one, a time frame for overcoming the obstacles and roadblocks. This separates the men and women from the boys and girls, because it's so easy to say, "Someday I'm going to open a restaurant," or "Someday I'm going to spend more time with the kids," or "Someday I'll realize my search for spiritual self-fulfillment." It could be any day or never. Once the time frame of a year or less is there, you have to work on the goal. It's concrete, it's written down, it's not idle conversation any more.

Finally, write down the advantages of achieving the goal, or, "what good things will happen to me if I reach my goal." If you can't list some positive things that will result, then something's the matter with the goal. Most important, you have to want, passionately want, to achieve the goal. You have to work at it steadily and check your progress as you go along. You must have an absolute commitment to the goal. That's where so many people fall down, in my opinion. Sure they would like to have the goal, but struggling for it through thick and thin isn't their idea of fun. How much better to go through a little hocus-pocus, thinking it's the substitute for achieving the goal. Paul's method clarifies the goal. After that it's achievable with commitment and unflinching labor.

Here is one example from my life. While I was doing motivational speaking – remember, motivational speakers are paid a lot – I treated myself to a new Lincoln and a new suit with two pairs of pants. It was early in the morning and my lips were sticky. I smoked Camel cigarettes, and in those days they had no filter. I'd just pulled that new Lincoln out of the driveway, lit a cigarette and guess what? I fumbled around with the lighter and glowing ash fell on my coat, burning a hole in it.

Here am I with a two-pant suit, and I burned a hole in the coat! Now I'm trying to beat the fire out with one hand and get the cigarette out of my mouth with the other. Finally I pulled the cigarette off my lips and the cigarette took some of the skin with it. Ouch! I was so distracted with all of this action that I couldn't drive the car and it plunged into a ditch. I wasn't hurt and the car wasn't hurt but I could have injured or even killed somebody or caused a lot of property damage.

All this happened about a block from home. My kids heard the car go into the ditch. They thought it was hilarious.

"Good thing you didn't run into the back of a school bus. We'd have every kid in the neighborhood running around with those white colored brace things around their necks."

Well, the kids thought it was funny but the accident awakened me to the dangers of smoking.

So I decided then and there to stop smoking. What were the obstacles? I wrote them down. There were a lot, namely all the times I wanted a cigarette. I had a cigarette in the morning with coffee, after leaving the house, with lunch, with a cocktail, after dinner, after sex, while working, or watching TV.

How would I overcome these many obstacles? I decided that the first way to overcome them was realizing that cigarettes were addictive, sure, but that smoking and its paraphernalia of cartons, packs, individual cigarettes, matches, and lighters was partly a kind of oral gratification and motor satisfaction in that it kept me busy with my hands. Next I wrote down the methods I'd use to break the smoking habit. I would throw out the cigarettes so none of them would be lying around to tempt me. But I'd keep the matches and lighter in my shirt pocket along with a package of gum and a little paper listing the advantages I'd realize if I kicked the habit.

Next I wrote down the time frame, one month. That was a tough one, but I was determined. It was easy to write out the advantages for me on the full sheet, with summaries on the paper in my pocket. I'd avoid accidents, stop burning holes in my clothes, have no yellow nicotine stains on my fingers, better breath, and more money to save or spend on other things.

Every time I used to reach for a cigarette I'd keep my hands busy reaching for that lighter, gum, and the condensed list. I'd pop the gum into my mouth, giving me the oral gratification. I'd read over the list at the same time. The people I was with sometimes thought the activity was a little strange. Usually I could explain it, but I'll leave to your imagination how I dealt with it after sex. The program worked and I stopped smoking almost immediately.

Now to wind up this discussion and this chapter: a lot of well-meaning people will tell you to visualize the result you want.

Every good selling manual or self-improvement program tells you that. Visualization is good. I've used it myself. For example, when I decided I wanted a Rolls Royce, I went to the dealer, got a brochure, cut out a photo of a Rolls and pinned it up on my office wall. In odd moments I looked at the photo and said to myself, "There's my car."

"That's my car," I'd say, whenever anybody asked about the photo.

"Nice car, where is it?"

"I don't have it yet, though having it is a goal I'm working toward."

But, and this is important, I was using the SMI system to move toward that goal. In other words, visualizing something is next to useless without a plan for achieving it.

• • •

Now you know how valuable "gate selling" and the SMI system were for me. After leaving motivational speaking and doing a few small selling jobs around Seattle, I found great success in selling car washes in Canada.

Chapter Six

Selling in Canada and an Invention I Couldn't Patent

How did I get into the car wash sales business in Canada? I emigrated to Canada. In the 1960s it was no big deal to cross the border and set up a business. A good friend who was building and selling Robo Car Washes asked me to come up from Seattle and help him. I'd left motivational speaking, I'd just finished selling out a big complex in the Seattle suburb of Kirkland, Yarrow Bay Apartments, and was looking for something to do.

What really appealed to me was buying and selling real estate. I never forgot what Granddad said, "Go buy corner lots in growing cities." Vancouver, British Columbia, was growing. Here was an opportunity to buy a property that was a drug on the market, get the proper zoning, overhaul it with a new car wash and gas station, and resell it. Everybody would profit. I wasn't so much interested in the car wash business itself. We didn't operate the car washes, although we retained some control over them, as you'll see. We sold the franchises and worked out the real estate deals while other people ran the car washes and the gas stations.

Here's how we did it. We'd drive around Vancouver, scouting locations for a new combined car wash and gas station. Sometimes we'd find a sizeable lot with a rundown building on it, yet it was in a high traffic area. Usually we'd discover a gas station, small and a little shabby, property not realizing its potential, given the traffic. We'd tell the oil company that owned it, "Look, you aren't doing well at this location, so sell us the lot for what little it's worth now." The company did.

In a typical deal, the company next made whatever improvements it wanted to the old gas station. We built the car wash, then sold the whole package - Robo, refurbished station, and lot - back to the company. We told the companies, "You'll make a lot more money," and they did. Or we could sell the package to somebody else, an individual who wanted an oil company franchise. We proved once again the old cliché about the three most important things in real estate, "Location, location, location."

Right away I learned that something else, land use control, or zoning, was just as important as location. In an urban area you had to have the correct land use situation. Just because there was an old gas station or a gimcrack building on a property zoned commercial didn't mean that you could waltz in and build a new or improved gas station and a car wash there. A better station and a car wash were bound to draw more traffic than the old structure attracted. Why else would anybody want to build or rebuild the gas station and car wash? There was sensitivity to traffic density in Vancouver.

The city traffic engineer was the key man in the zoning process. He went to the location, studied the traffic volume and traffic flow, the street widths, the necessary curb cuts, and all that, and made a recommendation regarding the impact on the surrounding community. If his decision for a building permit was positive, usually it breezed through the zoning commission. The city council generally accepted the zoning commission's recommendation without much investigation.

In one instance I knew how to keep things moving by catering to the traffic engineer's recreational proclivities, let's say. It happened after we'd bought a lot right in downtown Vancouver. Nobody could believe it, that we'd bought that property for a gas station and car wash. It was the best possible location, but because it was already a high density, high traffic area there was some concern about cars running in and out of there all day long. It was on Robson Street, one of the most fashionable streets in Vancouver.

The location was first rate but we were struggling without a building permit. There were delays and delays. Now I knew from a fairly long acquaintance that our friend, the traffic engineer, loved to gamble. So I took him to Las Vegas for a weekend, just on a lark, with no mention of our delayed permit, of course. It wasn't too long after the Las Vegas weekend that we got our building permit.

The car wash business taught us the importance of carefully calculating the numbers. Our theme was, "Free car wash with a fill-up." We figured that our car washes could give a free wash to anybody who bought a minimum number of gallons *and* filled their tank at the adjacent station. We pioneered that idea. A lot of people watched us and said, "You can't do this. You're going to go broke. You can't give away a car wash to people who buy gas. People will fill their tanks at the cheapest station in town. Then they'll drive over to one of your Robo stations, buy a half gallon of gas to refill their tanks, and demand a free car wash."

We'd thought of that ploy, so we weren't giving away washes to just anyone who bought gas. We gave away washes only to those who bought the minimum amount, say ten gallons, plus filled their tanks full at the same time. To put it another way, if you bought only ten gallons but didn't fill your tank, no free wash. If it took only eight gallons to fill your tank, no free wash.

The oil companies loved us. They wanted a Robo Car Wash next door because people would drive around until they were sure they needed at least ten gallons of gas. Then they'd stop in, fill their tanks, and get the little chit giving them a free wash.

Some people paid for washes without buying gas, and for them we had special promotions. For instance we had lots of cute girls dressed in pert uniforms. The men liked that. When people stopped in to get a wash, we gave them a sticker that they could put in their back window. Those stickers gave us a lot of advertising for the cost of the sticker. When people came in for a wash, if they were displaying the sticker, we gave them a free vacuuming job. A free car wash or a reduced price car wash with gas, and those other promotions, are pretty standard now.

Another way we sold the property and franchise was to interest a prospective owner in the potential increase in the property's value.

"We know that it's going to be expensive to clear this lot and put up a new station or improve the old one and build a car wash too. The lot's in a prime location. In later years the land may be worth much more."

If the buyer was an individual we'd say "The land value should

Young women at Robo Car Washes wore eye-catching costumes when the weather was nice. Men liked those outfits. They helped us sell more Robo locations too. From Robo News, June-July, 1969

soar, but even if the land doesn't increase much in value, you've built a business that your children and grandchildren will have. They can operate that business and make a living from it."

The station on Robson Street is a prime example of rising values. It's gone now. The land value increased so much that a new owner demolished it and put up a high-rise.

Now for that invention of mine which I couldn't patent. It happened this way: when we opened a new Robo Car Wash we'd have candy and balloons for the kids, coffee for the grownups, and soft drinks for everybody. Sometimes we'd put a searchlight in the drive so that people could find the business by following the searchlight. Then one day a customer of ours who already had a station and Robo opened his second gas station and Robo. He had free stuff and a searchlight at the old location and the new location.

Then it hit me: whenever a new Robo opened, why not have a searchlight panning the sky at every existing Robo, as well as the promotional items at every existing Robo? It was a new idea, though like a lot of new ideas, it had a precedent. The great thing about it was that it worked. We went searchlight crazy. We looked for searchlights as far away as Bellingham, in Washington state across the border. We even went to Seattle, renting searchlights. We had every searchlight in captivity.

There's a good story about the searchlights. Remember that this was the nineteen sixties and that any adult of a certain age, especially in Canada, remembered the "blitz." The "blitz" was the name that Londoners and other English urbanites gave to the German air attacks of the 1940s. The "blitz" may be small potatoes compared to later bomb damage but it was serious enough then. When the German bombers appeared overhead the air defense crews switched on their searchlights to find the bombers so that the anti-aircraft crews on the ground could aim at them. The searchlights lit up the London sky just as, one night, our Robo searchlights were lighting up the skies over Vancouver.

That night we Robo folks were up in the Blue Horizon Hotel, in its rooftop dining room, watching ten or twelve of our searchlights roaming the sky. We were enjoying the display, I especially, because it was my idea. Some newcomer to town was sitting near us at the bar.

"What the hell is going on?" he asked. "Are we having some kind of 'blitz' here or what?"

"Naw, it's just another of those damn Robo car washes," said a guy at the other end of the bar.

We had a good laugh. It was another fun part of being a salesman. Nowadays, when a new location of a chain opens, it's common to have promotions at all other locations. It's an invention I couldn't patent, but I'm proud of it.

I got much more out of that job besides satisfaction and laughs.

We made good money buying marginal properties and selling them at market rates. The money allowed me to buy my ranch in California, to give the kids a place to play, learn about horses and cows, and grow up with a knowledge of something besides urban living. We received a lot of favorable publicity in the Vancouver *Sun*. I became the Robo distributor for Western Canada.

At the end of our stint we had 15 car washes in Vancouver, and something like 126 all over Western Canada, in the provinces of Alberta and Saskatchewan as well as in British Columbia. I met the head of the McDonald's hamburger chain for Western Canada, and sold him on the same redevelopment idea. We used our proven techniques for buying, rezoning, and reselling properties for the McDonald's locations.

• • •

"Well," you are asking, "if real estate selling was what you wanted to do, and you were doing it, why aren't you in Canada today, selling real estate?"

I'll tell you in one word: government. Back then we paid all the usual taxes, and they were plenty high in Canada, but there was no capital gains tax on real estate sales. The federal government in Ottawa looked at all of the commercial property transactions in Canada's boom cities, and decided to levy a heavy tax on the difference we made between buying and selling those properties. We paid all the appropriate taxes already, but this was a new one. It took a big whack out of our income. So we decided that we were reaching market saturation anyway, and moved on.

That's the way governments always think. They think, '"Here's an activity that's laying lots of golden eggs for private individuals. Let's tax it more and get some of those golden eggs for the government." Governments always calculate their projected income on the basis of the private activity remaining at the same level as before the tax. In my experience that's hardly ever true. A new tax discourages business activity, and the government doesn't make the money it thought it would. In our case, we dropped the goose that was laying those golden eggs and got out.

• • •

The Robo Car Wash business led straight to my next venture, modular homes. It happened this way: In Seattle I'd been friends with Jack Anderson, who went north to Vancouver and operated a car dealership. We maintained our shared interest in car sales and service.

Jack's dealership had a lot set aside to sell these modulars, Carolin Homes. He did so well selling the houses, mostly vacation homes at first, that he got excited about the future of modular homes and bought into the company. He left the car business and recruited me to be the salesman for Carolin Homes.

Before we get into my role in this company, I want to take a detour to make a point about how business acumen often helps improve people's lives. Jack Mills, the founder of Carolin Homes, was already balding and a little paunchy while in his thirties, but there was nothing flaccid about his brain. In the late 1960s he saw the so-called trailer park was past the fad stage and that people were moving ever larger, wider trailers onto them as permanent residences. These trailers were never towed behind a car, but arrived on big flatbed trucks and after unloading never went anywhere.

But there were at least three problems with the trailers and the trailer parks. The lots were small, which made for minimum privacy and maximum noise. Local zoning ordinances often forced the trailer parks into low, scrubby land that nobody else wanted for private homes. The new trailers betrayed their heritage as travel trailers: they were narrow, with small windows, miniaturized kitchens and baths, and such gimmicks as fold-away tables to maximize the cramped floor space.

The modular home industry responded to the trailer park - trailer problem with bigger houses built from standard components and trucked to their destinations. The goal was to combine off-site construction, portability, and uncomplicated setup on the buyer's lot. It wasn't an easy goal to reach. Some houses weren't sturdy enough to stand the trip well, while other designs were stronger but assumed that the buyer had the skill to do most of the finishing work himself. Then there was competition from established businesses that sold pre-cut lumber and some pre-assembled components in a package for final assembly on the lot.

While Jack Mills mulled over all these issues, he confronted another problem: Canada's short house construction season. Rain in southern British Columbia and snow everywhere else made for a summer construction window that opened late and closed early. We're not talking Florida or South Texas here.

Jack's genius took the two problems - getting the modular houses right and the short construction season - and made one great opportunity out of them. In the summer of 1971, he founded Carolin Homes with the idea of combining a strongly-built, completely finished house with multiple transportation options and a rapid, careful setup on the purchaser's lot. The only on-site work was easy to do in the short summer. It involved pouring the foundation, putting in the plumbing up to its connection with the fittings in the modular home, and bringing in the electric power. Our dealers handled all that, working from plans we provided.

Did Jack Mills start right away to build these dream homes? You bet not! He began with motels, bunkhouses and small apartments that nobody was likely to live in very long. All the while he studied how to improve the design, until he arrived at a monocoque type house construction where all the parts of the unit such as the framing, the plywood sheets, the drywall and other components formed an interlocking, mutually reinforcing structure. The resulting house stood up to the stresses of moving and to Canada's harsh weather conditions. It's similar to the unibody construction of most of today's cars and many other light vehicles. Jack worked with architects to develop designs that were real houses, not contraptions that looked like the overgrown grandchild of a travel trailer.

Jack's inspiration was a godsend for Canadian homeowners. They could choose from fourteen models, each with a variety of interior finishes, carpeting, and colors. They could have the whole package shipped to the prepared lot at a price cheaper than on-site construction with an absolute minimum of bother. Jack's clearheaded thinking led him to a huge old World War II bomb

Here I am, about 1972, "checking" the work at a Carolin Home on the assembly line. Most likely I'm thinking, "Yes, they really have themselves some two-by-fours there," as this was more a publicity shot than anything else. The man in the background to my right is actually working. The distance between us gives an idea of the generous size of this modular home.

factory in New Westminster, a Vancouver suburb. The old factory was near the Frazier River, a railroad and a highway, so that the finished units could travel by water, rail, or a combination of transportation modes. The business quickly moved from vacation homes to year-round dwellings.

Another thing Mills learned from the car industry was to build on an assembly line, but not to try for complete vertical integration. Handling everything from manufacturing cabinets and plumbing to construction and sales was just too much for one organization. So he used established suppliers and standard kitchen and bath equipment. All the components went into the home at the right moment in a marvel of "just-in-time" assembly. The assembly line was another wonder. As Mills perfected it, construction began with two truck trailers pulled side by side. The carpenters and plumbers built the home as a unit on the beds of both trailers. When the home was finished it was "sawed in half" lengthwise, as we said, but really the decoupling was built into almost all of the home. Then, typically, a tractor truck hooked up each trailer with one half the house on it, and hauled it to the site.

At the site each truck pulled its trailer level with the prepared foundation. The trailers tilted inward, toward each other, and each half of the house slid off the trailer and onto the foundation. The carpenters and plumbers clipped and wired everything together, the local power people turned on the juice, and the home was ready.

Where did I come in? As general sales manager, selling franchises to dealers. Jack Mills wisely stayed out of direct sales but instead recruited dealers to do the selling to the public. That decision was in tune with his view that nobody was well enough informed to handle all aspects of a business like his, so he left selling to experienced dealers. My job was to get the dealers. It wasn't hard work. I used the Yellow Pages of the cities and towns throughout British Columbia to pinpoint the travel trailer and mobile home sales people. I'd invite them to come in and look over the factory, where we had the capacity for fifty homes under construction at the same time.

Before long we were getting referrals from dealers we'd already signed. A dealer, say, in Prince George would refer a dealer in, for instance, Prince Rupert, because they sold the same brand of mobile home. The Prince Rupert dealer would then come down and look us over. If there was a difficult phase to all of this it was writing up the sales agreements, the contracts, running the credit checks, and in the end, deciding if a particular dealer was right for us. We gave every dealer an exclusive territory.

To make sure that I knew what was going on I got out on the factory floor and watched the homes being built. I went along on the setup runs with the trucks and trailers a few times to see that end of the job. I wanted to be fully informed in order to answer questions from motivated dealers.

I became more involved in the business than I intended, because Jack Anderson was supposed to brainstorm the sales operation. He got involved in other things connected with the business, while Jack Mills and his construction boss were tied up with the production end. In fact I became a partner and ended up overseeing the whole show. In addition, I'd talk to the women buyers when they came to the factory to choose carpet colors, styles, cabinets, and so on. Those conversations allowed me to refine our interior finishing options.

It was great fun. We all worked in harness, and we did well. We got our financing from the Royal Bank of Canada on favorable terms. Ours was the first industry of its type that they'd financed, but we convinced them that we were riding the wave of the future, which we were. But at the same time we were growing restless, and ready to move on.

We'd already gone public. We held a big reception for the major stockbrokers in the Vancouver Stock Exchange. There were at least thirty-five of them in a large paneled meeting room in one of the hotels. I ran it, and made sure that we had lots of charts and photos on easels, to show them just how well we were doing. They agreed to sell our stock, raising more capital for us. Then a wealthy doctor from Vancouver Island looked us over and asked to buy us out. We agreed. I was in that business for about a year.

• • •

My next, and as it turned out, last sales venture in Canada was selling video games. My partner was Ehrenfried Liebich. You'll meet him again in the next chapter. At the time small computers were just coming in, and so were computer games like the early Pac-Man and Donkey Kong. The inventor of Donkey Kong didn't patent it, so anyone was free to produce a variant.

That's what we did. We arranged for a company in San Jose to manufacture the video games and the sometimes round, sometimes octagonal wooden tables that went with them. The company shipped them to us in Canada. The game was in a recess in the middle of the table. The player sat at the table, put a quarter in a slot of a standard coin holder and played the game. It cost us about $500 to make and ship the games. We sold them for around

That's me again, addressing a meeting of the leading stockbrokers of the Vancouver, British Columbia stock exchange, after we decided to take Carolin Homes public. The exchange listed our stock, we raised a good chunk of capital, and then sold the business.

$3,000. The difference wasn't all profit, naturally, but it was tidy enough for us.

Here's how we operated. We'd have a group of attractive young women go around to bars, lounges, some restaurants, or any other likely location for the games. They'd ask the owner of each establishment if they would be interested in having this exciting new game in their place of business, a game that would attract their patrons and keep them there ordering more food and drinks while

The Toronto office of our video games business, Can-Am Agency. We also provided big screen TVs.

they played the game. The young women would also point out that the game would be installed free of charge and that the owner would receive 50 percent of the receipts. A lot of business owners got on board.

Soon we'd have ten contracts in hand, covering a fairly compact area that was easy to service. Then we'd go to a person we'd already identified as a potential franchisee, interested in buying and servicing the machines. We'd say, "Here are ten contracts, now buy the machines from us, we'll install them and set them up, and you'll start making money." Few of the franchisees had $30,000 just sitting around, waiting to be invested, so we arranged with the banks to finance them.

Our main headquarters was in Toronto. I went to the manager of the Toronto branch of the Bank of Montreal and persuaded him to advertise the games in the lobby of the bank. The ad stated that

That's me once again on the left, dressed in the height of 1970s fashion, with high top, mid-heel shoes, flared trousers, a wide lapel jacket with patch pockets, and a wide tie. My hair was in the mode, too. I'm congratulating the Toronto branch manager of the Bank of Montreal for arranging loans to distributors of our video games.

the bank would finance those who were interested in this excellent business opportunity. It worked. We made money, the bank made money, and the franchisee made money.

If I say so myself, this was a big deal. Our headquarters were in Toronto but we operated all over Canada and had outlets in Vancouver and Calgary, plus offices in London, Paris, and Dusseldorf, Germany, in addition to the manufacturing operation in San Jose. It was hard work but we did very well. We used some variations in our basic sales theme when the circumstances were right. We sold those games all over the place, including such customers as the British Columbia ferry system. Finally the incessant work and the problems with the business became too much and we sold it.

• • •

Before I describe all that I'd like to put you in touch with another man who will figure in future chapters, Jess Kellogg. Jess and I knew each other from my parts department days at my uncle's Ford dealership. Jess operated a body shop near the dealership. We arranged with him to do our body repair work and he bought his Ford parts from us.

Jess owned a boat. He was - and still is - a large, powerful man with a sunny disposition that attracted the opposite sex. I was between marriages for the later part of our friendship in Seattle, so I enjoyed Jess' positive attitude toward getting the girls. Though he was big and strong, Jess was light on his feet and a great dancer. Once we had the girls, Jess could deal with any guys who tried to take them away from us or otherwise give us a hard time. Our boating life was nonstop wine, women, and song. Jess bought a new Cadillac convertible every year, and that sure didn't hurt us with the girls.

Jess helped out with another venture, the "Wunderbug." I'll explain. Back in the early days of the Volkswagen beetles some people had the idea of putting a different hood and grille configuration on them to make them look like another car. I knew a man who gave his daughter a VW but had it converted to look like a miniature Mercedes. He figured that a big hood and grille out front was safer than the sloping VW hood.

Mercedes wasn't the only variation. My original partner in the car washes, Lou Dallas, was in business with people who were turning out VWs with modified parts to look like 1940 Fords. They called their cars the Wunderbug. They were making the simulated 1940 Ford stampings in the same factory that made the Robo parts. Lou brought me into the business. The problem was, we'd take orders as they came in from people who had seen a Wunderbug around or who had seen our modest ads, and wanted one for themselves.

"Well, we're not going to do very much with those onesies and twosies," we said to ourselves.

That's when I had an idea.

"Why don't we, if we are really proud of the product, go to the Volkswagen dealers and sell them on the idea of buying these modified cars to sell at their dealerships?"

"They'll never go for that," everybody said.

"Well, let me try."

I went to the main distributor for California and the West Coast, who also had a dealership, and convinced him that these modified VWs could be sold on the showroom floor. He allowed us to go to the dealers. So we went out to each dealer area, hosted a dealer meeting, and all the dealers from that area would come. We had one of our Wunderbugs there so that they could see that it was a fine job with excellent fit and finish. We sold every dealer fifteen or twenty at a time.

That's when Jess entered the picture. We needed a man who knew body work and could put the cars together on practically an assembly line basis. He did the modifications and repainting right on the pier at Oakland. The dealers bought the cars from Volkswagen, then sent them to us. We modified them, sent them back to the dealers with a charge for our work, and they put them on the showroom floor along with their regular cars.

Sure, the Wunderbugs cost more, but the different shape and appearance were novel and exciting, and they sold well. Sadly, we found that novelties last only so long, especially fairly expensive ones like cars. Jess reconfigured 500 or so Wunderbugs before the newness and attractiveness wore off, but by then I was working on video games.

• • •

The video game business proved to be nerve wracking. It seemed like I was almost constantly in the air, flying to one or the other of our outlets, flying back, then flying on to another one. There were problems. If the coin machine in one game wouldn't work and if it was in warranty, we'd have to have it repaired. If a circuit board went flooy and the game wouldn't work the guy with the contract for that restaurant or whatever would call us to fix it, and he'd want a replacement game yesterday.

Other problems plagued us. Toronto was not the best place for my arthritis. Then there was Canada in general. It was much too cold for too long. Worse than that, in Vancouver a few of our games were dragged out of their bars or other locations and thrown back in the alley, or out on the street. The owners were too intimidated to tell us anything about who had destroyed our games or why.

We had a clue about what was going on when I got a call from a man in Vancouver who said that he was with such-and-such a company that was in the vending machine business. Since we were also in the vending machine business, he said, we should have a meeting to discuss a potential business arrangement. He strongly hinted that it would be unwise for me to reject his idea of a meeting. It didn't take too much intellectual horsepower to realize that he was behind those video games that wound up in the alleys or on the streets. Nor did it take a giant intellect to understand that this business arrangement he wanted was a cut of our business. This guy was probably not directly connected to the Mafia but he was no shrinking violet either, because he later went to prison in Arizona for having a man shot and killed.

I went to the restaurant he designated and chose a booth in full view of the other tables and booths. The boss man came in with another fellow, muscular but not looking like the sharpest pencil in the box. We all sat down with me in the middle and the muscleman at one end of the booth. I noticed that Mr. Tough Guy, the not-so-bright one, was wearing shorts, a matter I used to my advantage. I knew that my partner, Ehrenfried, then in California on business, could deal with this attempt on our profits better than I could. So I decided to stall.

"I don't know what to tell you," I said, "except that we're not interested in partners. That I'm sure of."

It wasn't what they wanted to hear. So I thought, I'm leaving town anyway. We'll see what these guys are made of. I raised my voice, my voice carries anyhow, so that everyone in the restaurant would know what was going on.

"I don't know what you guys are all about," I said in a loud voice. "I don't appreciate our machines being thrown out in the street. If there's going to be any rough stuff, let's start it right now!"

I jammed my bony knees as hard as I could into the tough guy's bare thigh. He let out a yelp and jumped out of the booth.

"Ouch, my leg!" he wailed.

I jumped out of the booth too.

"I think this meeting is over. Goodbye," I said.

I made a quick exit from the restaurant, disappeared in a hurry, and caught the next plane for Toronto. I wouldn't behave like that today any more than I'd fly to the moon, but then I was comparatively young and very foolish. Anyway, Ehrenfried came back, apologized for my behavior to our wannabe partners, and cut a deal with the boss man. We were closing out our Vancouver business in any case, so I don't think that the boss man ever got anything.

Back in Toronto, things were no better than they were before. Much to my later good fortune, Jess and I stayed in touch during our post-Wunderbug years. I kept telling him how much I wanted to get out of the video game business and get out of Toronto. I told him that we'd about saturated the video game market.

Meanwhile a mutual friend of ours in Canada, Don Harris, had moved to Cabo San Lucas on the tip of Mexico's Baja California peninsula. He sold condominiums for the Costamex Company. They were some of the first condos in Cabo. He hired Jess as a salesman and all-round second in command.

"Why don't you come down here for a vacation?" Jess said in a telephone call. "Get out of that Toronto environment for a while."

Now then, my daughter Lisa was visiting me in Toronto as she always did during vacations. I had complete charge of her since she was about six years old. You'll remember Lisa. She was the one who told me to stop my latest lecture on how daughters should behave. "Tell me the ending," she said, "and I'll tell you if I need to hear the beginning and the middle."

Lisa and I dug the Maserati out of the snow, drove to the airport and flew to Cabo. It was 80 degrees there. We loved it. Early into our visit Jess suggested that I should come to Cabo and work for his company. One day we borrowed Jess's dune buggy and drove to Todos Santos for lunch. Todos Santos was then a quaint village up the Pacific coast from Cabo San Lucas. While we drove back, Lisa launched into a sales pitch for Jess's idea.

"Dad, you look happier driving this little car than your brand new Rolls Royce. Why don't you listen to Jess, sell your company, come down here and sell real estate? In Toronto you're too far away. I hardly ever see you, we don't go to the ranch, never have fun, never ride the horses. In case you haven't noticed, I'm growing up. I can see you more often and you'll have less pressure."

I went back to Toronto following the week in Cabo, and Lisa returned to boarding school in Vancouver. After about three months more in Toronto, I threw in the towel, sold out, and one day turned up on Jess's doorstep. Before I tell you about that experience, I want you to meet an amazing man, Bernard Cornfeld.

The Chateau Pelle de Cornfeld, Bernard "Bernie" Cornfeld's castle in the south of France. As head of Investor's Overseas Services, Bernie made a fortune and lived an opulent life, moving between palatial residences while surrounded by beautiful women. It was my good fortune to know him and to stay at his Beverly Hills mansion from time to time.

Chapter Seven

Bernie

Here I want to break the chronology again to tell you about Bernard Cornfeld, the most extraordinary man I've ever known. Bernie is not a household name now, but he was very well known, loved, and hated in the late nineteen fifties, sixties, and early seventies. Back then, he controlled about 2.5 billion dollars in investments. Knowledgeable people estimated his net worth at $100 million, well before our funny-money inflated dollar cut the value of such a huge fortune. Of course $100 million isn't chicken feed, even now.

Bernie owned a castle in France, a huge house in Beverly Hills, and big houses, apartments, or condos in Paris, London, New York, Geneva and elsewhere. A fleet of jets waited on his orders. He owned cars, exotic pets, and all sorts of other property. Then there were the women. He never went anywhere without eight or ten of the most beautiful women in tow. His charisma and magnetism, especially for women, were absolutely amazing.

But I'm getting ahead of the story. Let's begin with a look at Bernie's life up to the time I met him. Bernie was born in 1927 in Istanbul, Turkey, of all places. His father was Romanian and his mother Russian. His father suffered an accident that ended his acting and theater career in Turkey. When Bernie was about three they moved to the United States and eventually settled in New York, where Bernie grew up. His father died when Bernie was a kid. His mother worked as a nurse to support the family of five boys, four of them sons of Bernie's dad and his first wife. I guess you could describe their life in Brooklyn, with its strong intellectual and socialist component, as shabby-genteel. Bernie became an Eagle Scout.

Right after World War II Bernie joined the merchant marine, then graduated from Brooklyn College in 1950 with a BA in psychology. He knocked around a bit. He worked for B'nai B'rith in Philadelphia for a time, and called himself a "social worker" but he was more like a youth counselor. He claimed an MA from Columbia University but I don't know if he actually got one. His pals of the era remembered a guy who was a little rumpled, and liked what for young men without much money were nifty cars, such as a yellow Chevy convertible. He liked girls too, and dreamed of making lots of money.

Bernie was in the investment business for a while, then went to Paris in 1955 without a firm idea of what to do next. Soon, though, he took advantage of four related circumstances unique to his time.

The first was a long boom in the stock market that began in the mid 1950s and lasted until about 1969. Sure, there were setbacks and selloffs, but the market always recovered and went on to new highs. The second was the rise of mutual funds from practically nothing. Investors bought shares of mutual funds rather than stocks in individual companies and trusted in savvy managers to buy into companies whose stock would go up. Everybody understood that the savvy mutual fund managers charged commissions for making shrewd investments, but the mutual fund investors counted on the increase in the value of the mutual fund shares to more than cover the commissions.

Third, real incomes rose so that people who were just getting by right after World War II had more than enough money to support their lifestyles. They were able to invest their surplus in stocks and, most important for Bernie, in mutual funds. The fourth circumstance was the development of offshore companies, companies set up partly to avoid U.S. laws and government regulations.

Let's talk about those offshore companies and U.S. laws and regulations for just a moment. Lots of people think that it's just horrible for a company to dodge U.S. laws and regulations. They believe that our laws and regulations are wonderful, and that companies who go offshore are out to make a fast buck, fleece investors, or do other bad things. Some offshore companies are crooked, of course, but what the people who love the U.S. government's regulations don't get is that business taxes are high and that business regulations are onerous. Some companies go offshore just to cut the cost of doing business.

• • •

Bernie began by arranging with the Dreyfus Fund, a hotshot mutual fund of the era, to sell shares of Dreyfus to Americans overseas. Overseas Americans were of two types, service people and expatriates. Neither group had very many well-to-do people in it, but that was O.K. There were enough people with modest incomes in both groups who were willing to buy Dreyfus Fund shares on the installment plan. Bernie's salesmen worked hard because they made commissions up front on the value of the shares when fully paid, not on the installments as they dribbled in. Everybody figured that sales of Dreyfus Fund shares would rise along with the stock market and more than offset the commissions.

Bernie took advantage of offshoring to incorporate his company in Panama, where regulations scarcely existed, and move his headquarters out of Paris, where the French government could be fussy. He moved it to Geneva, where the Swiss government was a lot less fussy. He called his company Investors Overseas Services (IOS).

In part the offshoring was to make it difficult or impossible for the U.S. Internal Revenue Service to find out how much money anybody connected with IOS, sellers or buyers, was making. The Internal Revenue Service expected every U.S. citizen making so much as a dime overseas to report that income to the IRS and pay taxes on it. Personally, I think that rule was, and is, absurd. Any U.S. citizen overseas making money, is making money according to the laws and protection of the government he's living under. The U.S. government isn't helping him one bit. Any of these earnings that find their way back to the U.S. are pure gravy for the U.S. economy. Uncle Sam, leave our overseas moneymakers alone!

Meanwhile, IOS wasn't making a lot of money on Dreyfus shares, buying them from Dreyfus and reselling them. The salesmen used high-power techniques, mostly of Bernie's devising, to sell. They were doing all right on their commissions, but the company wasn't. So Bernie set up his first mutual fund within the IOS. That made IOS a sort of holding company.

Bernie followed this with the Fund of Funds, designed to invest in other mutual funds. IOS got a reduced price from the mutual funds, because of its large-volume purchases. The mutual funds themselves took commissions on their sales to the Fund of Funds, a perfectly legitimate thing for them to do. But, Bernie figured, why shouldn't IOS be getting the commissions that the mutual funds were making?

So Bernie and his colleagues decided to create more of their own mutual funds to invest in. Their arrangement worked very well. The company then collected two commissions, one when the IOS-owned mutual funds sold shares in their funds to the Fund of Funds, and another when the Fund of Funds sold its shares to its customers.

It was a breathtaking money making machine. Bernie moved on to own banks and insurance companies. At one time IOS had fifty-five subsidiaries with investments in everything under the sun. Bernie's salesmen moved on, too, by selling to almost everyone under the sun, except in the U.S., where IOS couldn't do business. IOS became a global company and naturally it ran into trouble with some governments. It all got very complicated and it isn't part of my story to iron out all of IOS's problems.

About 1969 Bernie's empire began to totter and in 1970 he had to admit that IOS was in trouble. He and his board cast about for rescuers. Several people, including one of the Rothschilds, looked IOS over but either they didn't have the resources to dig IOS out of trouble or they didn't like the setup and associating themselves with it.

• • •

This is when I met Bernie, just before the troubles. My friend Ehrenfried, the co-owner of the video games business, liked girls as much as Bernie did. The girls liked Ehrenfried, too, though not because of his appearance. He was of middle height at best and wore a beard that made him look older, but he was a charmer. He attracted people because of his jovial, positive personality.

"Come on," Ehrenfried said one day, "there's somebody I want you to meet."

We were in Paris. He introduced us. I saw right away why Ehrenfried and Bernie hit it off. Bernie did not have Hollywood looks by any stretch of the imagination. He was about five feet five, balding and a little paunchy, and wore a beard. He spoke softly, almost in a whisper. Yet he had appealing ways about him. He wasn't fixated on money for itself. Money meant nothing to him except as a means to buy houses and other property, and have a great time.

He was generous to people. For instance, he might believe that some guy who was managing one of his houses, could do more. He'd give the guy a job and some shares of IOS, which wasn't publicly traded then. But everybody believed that IOS would be a good deal down the road, which it was, briefly.

With Bernie, every day was Christmas for some of the people he liked. He would load up a limousine with some of his ladies and take them to a department store. He'd tell them they could shop for half an hour and he would pay the bill. The smart ones made a beeline for the furs and diamonds. He sat in the limo until the time was up, smiling, laughing, and joking with the chauffeur. He really enjoyed visualizing those beautiful women rushing about the store, grabbing whatever they could. Or, he'd be with a group of friends, and a happy thought would occur to him.

"Let's go to Acapulco for the weekend!" he'd say on the spur of the moment. Off they'd go, with Bernie paying for the plane and the hotel rooms.

And then there were the girls. I don't mean girls who were pretty or cute, but astonishingly beautiful women who were actresses or the top models of whatever city he was in. Victoria Principal was one of his earlier conquests. It was a slow day if he didn't have at least half a dozen beauties hanging around. He liked to brag about bedding them all every day but we understood that there was usually a girl of the week or month and that the others were along for a free ride, out of curiosity, mostly.

In any case he drew women to him like iron filings to a magnet.

I know that's a cliché but it's true. He'd go into a restaurant and in ten minutes he'd have all the women around him, or at least all the women whose husbands or boyfriends weren't dragging them back to their tables. Once we were at an airport, going somewhere on a plane, and there was a girl Bernie liked who had a ticket to fly to see her mother. Bernie talked to her for a few minutes. To heck with mom! She got on the plane with us.

Sometimes the girls could be a distraction. One summer a group of us were at Bernie's castle in the south of France. Those beautiful models sat around the pool topless. I'd taken along some work to do but it was hard to concentrate with that show going on. Another time I was at Bernie's townhouse in Paris. Remember that Ehrenfried and I had video game offices here and there, including Paris. We made a deal with Bernie to use part of his Paris digs for an office when we needed it. The arrangement was informal.

"Sure! Come up and stay with me," he said.

Bernie kept the upper floors and we had the lower. One day I was struggling with some paperwork. There was a steady stream of beauties going up and down the stairs to and from Bernie's quarters. Elizabeth Taylor was one of them. I couldn't concentrate, thinking about being willing to take even as much as Bernie's leftovers. Finally I had to quit working.

Bernie liked to say that his love life represented the "joy of anarchy." Some of the "joy" went out of his love life after he became intimate with Lorraine Armbruster, one of those top fashion models. He got Lorraine pregnant. She wanted to get married. He didn't. Finally he gave in and the wedding was lavish, to put it mildly. Before he was married, he asked Ehrenfried's opinion of the idea. Ehrenfried advised him to be careful with the womanizing because Lorraine wasn't going to like it, she knew Bernie's habits and she would be looking out for any two-timing.

Bernie assured Ehrenfried that everything was going to be OK. I think it was only a short time after the wedding that Lorraine caught him in bed with another woman in their house. She reminded him that it wasn't her idea of keeping his marriage vows. They stuck it out for some time but Bernie kept playing around.

Lorraine decided that if Bernie had girlfriends, she was going to get a boyfriend. And she did. This guy had a home in Aspen, Colorado, and Lorraine went there to visit him while Bernie was on one of his trips. On that occasion Bernie, Ehrenfried, and I were all in New York City on business. We'd arranged to ride home in the same taxi after meetings with lawyers in town. We were riding back to Bernie's penthouse with Ehrenfried on one side, me on the other side, and Bernie in the middle.

Bernie had hired a private detective to keep tabs on Lorraine. He was pouting and stewing about this boyfriend.

Ehrenfried said something like, "Well, you know, Bernie, how can you be upset about Lorraine? We're going to a party tonight, we're going to have ten girls, you're going to try to take all ten of them to bed, how can you be upset with Lorraine?"

Bernie said, in all sincerity, huffing and puffing,

"But she's a mother!"

Couldn't argue with that.

The party Ehrenfried referred to was a Super Bowl party. We had a big screen TV and Bernie's ten girls were there. After the game was over the party was going really good, the music was on, and the girls were naked. What a recipe for a high time! Then the phone rang. It was Bernie's private detective telling him that Lorraine had just bought her boyfriend a brand-new Rolls Royce Corniche convertible. With Bernie's money. Ehrenfried and I were in the kitchen getting some pizza ready when Bernie whanged open the swinging door, ran in and began ranting at us. He was livid.

"What do you guys know about this? You must know about this, the boyfriend and the car!"

Of course we knew about the boyfriend but nothing about the Rolls Royce.

Bernie stormed out of the kitchen and got Lorraine on the phone, screaming at her over the phone. He was quiet most of the time but he did have a temper and he could scream and yell.

"Get on the plane!" he shouted. "I know all about this guy, you're coming to New York, get on the red-eye, bring Jessica!"

Jessica was their daughter, then four or five years old. We pled with Bernie not to go to the airport and have a confrontation. We begged him to wait until Lorraine got to the penthouse, and she and Jessica were settled in. Then they could talk the situation over calmly. Unfortunately that wasn't Bernie's style. He hired a limo and met Lorraine and Jessica at six in the morning. Back at the penthouse Ehrenfried and I were trying to clean up after the party and get everyone out of there. Lorraine and Jessica came in, all in tears because Bernie'd been yelling at them all the way from the airport.

Fortunately Bernie had gotten most of the mad out of his system so we were able to shut everything down more or less decorously and get some sleep. Soon Bernie and Lorraine left on a round-the-world tour to see if they could patch things up, taking along their entourage of maids, babysitters and other servants. I think they were gone three months.

About the time of their trip, Lorraine bought a house up the hill from Grayhall, Bernie's vast mansion in Beverly Hills. That was when things got out of hand or really comic, depending on your point of view. Lorraine painted her place pink and called it "Pinkhall." So now we had Grayhall and Pinkhall. Bernie was afraid that Lorraine would empty all of the massive old furniture out of Grayhall and take it to Pinkhall, so he hired a security guard. Lorraine decided that if Bernie had a security guard, she needed a bodyguard. Bernie concluded that if Lorraine had a bodyguard, he should have a bodyguard too.

Now there were two bodyguards and a security guard, with Bernie paying $100 a day to each one. Since they didn't really have anything to do, Lorraine's bodyguard came down to Grayhall and they sat around Grayhall playing backgammon. Eventually Bernie and Lorraine divorced but stayed friendly. Lorraine remarried and she and her new husband were welcome at Bernie's summer parties at his castle in France. Bernie went on being Bernie. "Polygamy is easier than monogamy and a lot more fun," was one of his favorite lines.

Back to the backgammon games and my younger daughter Lisa. I had a standing invitation to stay at Grayhall whenever I was in the Los Angeles area. When I could I brought Lisa along, and Bernie would have a nice suite waiting for us. Because backgammon was a two-person game one of the guards was always odd man out, and looking for a partner. The odd man out asked Lisa to play with him. If I say so myself, Lisa was bright and competitive and had studied backgammon, then a popular game among the rich and powerful. She agreed, so we put our bags in our rooms and went back downstairs.

"You really should let him win. Let him win," I suggested to Lisa as we walked down the stairs.

She wasn't about to, and of course she won.

• • •

Another story about Lisa and Grayhall is worth telling. During one of our visits Warner Bros. was filming their 1976 version of *A Star Is Born* starring Kris Kristofferson and Barbra Streisand. Kristofferson liked his beer and was drunk most of the time. Warner rented the downstairs of Grayhall. Grayhall had a huge great room with a monster pipe organ, the works.

In the movie the great room was supposed to be unfurnished so Bernie called in Bekins and had them take out all the furniture and put it in storage. One scene called for Kristofferson to show Streisand his enormous great hall then grab her hand and lead her up the curving stairs, meanwhile writing "I love you" backwards in spray paint on the wall by the stairs. It was a fairly intricate scene. Naturally they couldn't use Bernie's wallpaper so they had this special paint on the wall, and had everything else covered so that any overspray wouldn't damage the stairs or anything else. It all had to look correct, like a real house.

While they were setting up to shoot the scene Lisa and I were out shopping for groceries as we often did. Bernie was by then down to his last few million and sometimes short of cash. We had unloaded and put away the groceries. In the great room they were beginning to shoot, with the lights on and all that. Lisa was about thirteen. She stepped out from the kitchen into the great room. She had no idea what was going on except that there were some people standing around. There were always people standing around, hangers-on, people trying to get Bernie's attention, and the merely curious. What she noticed was this strange guy hustling up the stairs, meanwhile making a mess on the wall with spray paint.

Lisa pointed at Kristofferson and yelled, "He's going to get in trouble for that!" The director threw a fit. He was furious. He stopped the filming. It took the crews two days to get everything set up again. But as they hadn't warned Lisa or much of anyone else, they couldn't do anything except start over. We had a lot of fun in that house.

• • •

To return to Bernie's business issues and his difficulties with various governments.

Bernie liked to make us believe that he had sex on the brain but he was down-to-earth about business. One day he mentioned that he had a limousine he no longer needed. I thought it would be nice to tool around in that car so we began negotiating the price. He proved to be nobody's fool when it came to business. When I balked at a price he'd set on a "take it or leave it" basis he said, "That's the only car I've got that you can have sex in!" So I paid more for the car just because of his statement. Sex on the brain, maybe, but business on the brain when it mattered.

Bernie liked nothing better than combining business and pleasure. When he took IOS public he created about a hundred millionaires, at least on paper. He decided to celebrate. His idea of a proper celebration was to load one of his big planes to fly everybody who wanted to go to his castle in France. The castle staff was used to handling large numbers of people but a plane load of visitors was too much. Perhaps the chefs and servers were too stressed to be careful. The kitchen caught on fire in a big way, and the fire department had to be called in to put it out.

Moving on to the downfall of IOS, Bernie was called a lot of names, some of the more polite being swindler, cheat, and scam artist. I never believed any of that for a moment. Bernie never intended to hurt anyone or steal anything. He had his foibles but when he adopted the IOS slogan, "Do You Sincerely Want to be Rich?" he meant it. He was going to make all of his people and his investors wealthy. If you knew him you had to like him for his generosity and kindness.

Yet IOS collapsed and Bernie had to share some of the blame, but not all of it. The big problem was this: IOS started out as a sales organization primarily and stayed primarily a sales organization. Bernie was a good salesman himself and a great motivator of other sales people. He concentrated on that. He didn't pay enough attention to things like the general rules of the countries where he did business.

Here's an example: Bernie hired a lot of young people from the U.S. to work at his Geneva headquarters. They were full of animal spirits. They should have been given an orientation on local etiquette, because the Swiss were rather formal, reserved, and not overflowing with tolerant good humor. The young people would fake enrollment in a Swiss university, or they would "forget" to apply for a work permit, thereby dodging Swiss taxes. Bernie didn't condone any of it but he didn't have any program in place to deal with scofflaw employees. So the Swiss investigated IOS from top to bottom, found a lot of complicated deals, and put Bernie in prison for eleven months on charges of securities fraud.

Bernie got out of prison when actor George Hamilton and other friends raised a million dollars' bail. Better still, he finally got the money back with a little interest but other basic problems remained.

Bernie hired people to shape up IOS. They could only do so much, because Bernie wanted his huge 2.5 billion-dollar IOS to be his baby, just like it was in the late fifties when he was selling Dreyfus Fund shares. A business with fifty-five subsidiaries and 16,000 sales people – 16,000! – needed strict internal controls and strict accounting. But Bernie didn't think it was necessary. So IOS existed with practically no internal controls and with ramshackle accounting. Besides the lack of controls and poor accounting procedures, there were top people in IOS who took advantage of them to violate Bernie's trust. Bernie considered them close friends, made them rich, and would have done anything for them, yet they ran their own rackets within IOS to line their pockets.

Things came to a head in 1970 when the IOS board fired Bernie and looked around for a savior. As I've already mentioned, some people examined a bailout of IOS but decided either that the rescue operation was too big for them or that they didn't want to be associated with a company whose reputation had slipped so badly. That's when Robert Vesco stepped into the picture.

Vesco in some ways was everything that Bernie wasn't. He was a big man, and handsome in a B movie star way. He was a natural athlete but for years showed no interest in athletics except as a spectator. Then he found out that it would help him socially if he learned to play tennis. At the beginning he didn't know a tennis court from a trailer court or the business end of a tennis racket from the handle, but in short order he became an ace club player. He probably could have become a pro player in one of the major sports if he'd wanted to.

What Vesco wanted to do, though, was get rich. He had boundless drive, imagination, ambition, and ruthlessness, and an absolutely incredible analytical mind. In a series of complex maneuvers he used the fact that IOS had gone public to get together an important block of shares. He took over and let most of the company go to smash, allegedly. Meanwhile he supposedly siphoned off huge assets that the rightful owners couldn't claim because they had bought them in violation of their countries' currency exchange controls.

I was there at Grayhall when the problems with Vesco were serious, he was buying IOS shares, and Bernie's reputation was going into the tank. Bernie got Vesco on his big speakerphone and told him, "Bob, you're the one that sunk the company, you're the one who got us in trouble. How could you do this?" Vesco's comment was, "Bernie, you're the one that sold the people the stock."

Bernie blamed German bankers for selling IOS stock short, depressing its price, and thus making it ripe for a takeover. He claimed that the banks were mad because his aggressive salesmen took business away from them. There's some truth to that. There's also some truth to Vesco's observation that Bernie spent too much time with the girls and not enough time with his business.

I think what sank IOS was the end of the long boom in the stock market. Had Bernie run a tight ship and been ruthless with the people who betrayed him he might have weathered the storm. But Vesco took over with promises to save IOS. Instead he allegedly looted it, became a fugitive from U.S. Justice, and died in Cuba in 2007.

Bernie continued to have his troubles with government. He hated the Securities and Exchange Commission, which policed the stock market. He accused the SEC of illegally interfering with his business. The SEC returned the favor by hating Bernie and making as much trouble for him as possible.

The Internal Revenue Service and Bernie were not exactly friends, either. They had a running battle. During one of my visits to Grayhall a letter from the IRS arrived. Bernie opened it and started laughing. I said, "Bernie, you have a letter from the IRS and you're laughing?" It was a bill for $250,000. He was laughing over a statement at the bottom of the letter that read something like: "If you have paid the amount indicated, please disregard this invoice." Bernie laughed and said, "I haven't paid it. I won't pay it now, and I'm never going to pay it."

Bernie kept trying to make a business comeback. He and his friend Hugh Hefner of *Playboy* fame opened a restaurant that succeeded for a while. Then the in-crowd moved on as it always does. He tried real estate and movie making, even claimed he was going to buy MGM/UA, but nothing came of it. He had an idea for a new health food and wellness conglomerate that, among other things, would sell products to maintain men's sexual potency. *Forbes* magazine ran a story on it titled, "Do You Sincerely Want to Make Out," a parody of Bernie's "Do You Sincerely Want to be Rich" slogan.

• • •

I was involved in one of Bernie's ventures in real estate. It happened this way: for a time Howard Hughes, the reclusive billionaire, lived in the fabulous Xanadu Princess complex on Grand Bahama Island in the Bahamas. Later it was the Radisson Xanadu Beach Marina Resort. You may know it by that name.

The management of the Xanadu Princess let the hotel and its

Radisson Xanadu Hotel & Marina Resort, Freeport, Bahamas. From the Nosotros...Costamex magazine, vol. 2 (December 1989)

surroundings run down. Sure, they maintained the penthouse floor and the one below that Hughes and his entourage occupied. When Hughes moved out in 1976, most of the hotel was structurally sound but shabby and it wasn't drawing much of a tourist crowd.

The Bahaman government more or less took over the place, until it could get somebody to renovate the hotel. The government got Sir Freddie Laker, then the head of Laker Airways, interested. He rounded up some backers and, since he and Bernie were friends, brought Bernie into it. At the time Laker Airways was a budget airline that looked like it was going to be a permanent fixture on the transportation scene, the Queen of England had knighted Laker, and Bernie was Bernie.

Bernie and Sir Freddie discussed what to do with Xanadu. By that time I'd had a lot of experience in condo and timeshare sales in Mexico, so Bernie said, "I know this guy who can help us," and brought me in as one of a group of experts. I set up a meeting with the pertinent government officials and Bernie. They came to the Xanadu Princess dressed in suits. I remember one very proper lady, a very stern-looking woman with a high collar and lacy blouse. The Bahamas were once an English colony, and like a lot of ex-colonials, the woman and her fellow officials were more proper than the proper English.

Bernie was late. He was always late, in fact he had no more sense of time than he had of money. He missed planes. Once he showed up a day late for a speech he'd promised to make. On the day I'm discussing, he kept us waiting for two hours. I'd gone outside in the lobby to intercept him and ask him to apologize for his tardiness.

What I saw was a lot worse than lateness. He strolled into the lobby dressed in a sleeveless tank top and white pants rolled up to the knee. He was barefoot. A girl was with him, a girl dressed like she was going to be the main act at a strip club.

"Bernie, you can't go in there dressed like that," I said.

"Well, we're in the Bahamas. What's the big deal about this?"

"You can't bring her in there, dressed the way she is," I continued.

Now Bernie was getting testy, like I'm the sartorial police.

"She's my friend. By God, if they don't like it, that's too bad."

I took this photo of Bernie and one of his many girlfriends in 1976 at the Zanadu Princess Hotel in the Bahamas.

We walked in, with me tailing behind and thinking that this wasn't a good idea. Here were all the government officials sitting on one side of this long table, with their arms folded in front of them, glaring at us. They were looking at us like we were exotic birds that had flown out of a cage at the zoo. Needless to say, the meeting did not go well.

After that, when Sir Freddie's major backer learned that Bernie was involved, he balked. Meanwhile Bernie decided that he liked Xanadu and moved us in, and invited all sorts of people to visit, providing them with free rooms. He ran up a tab of $76,000. The rest of us got together and arranged a sale to my old company, Costamex, making sure that enough was included to pay some of Bernie's bill. Bernie liked to say that "It's hard having a reputation like mine to live down to." But sometimes he managed.

• • •

Bernie had so much trouble with making some of his ventures go because the federal government kept hounding him. It wanted to get him the worst way. To this day I believe that the government started the rumor that Bernie was involved in the drug trade. He wasn't so stupid. Meanwhile the phone company discovered that somebody at Grayhall was using a blue box. "Blue box" was a generic name for some gizmos used to bypass phone company safeguards and make free long distance calls. They were a fad among celebrities at the time. When the celebs were caught, all that the phone company or the government would do was say, "naughty, naughty, stop using the blue box, you naughty boy (or girl)."

Not so with Bernie. FBI agents conducted a full dress raid on Grayhall, looking for whatever they could find. They found a blue box. Bernie claimed to have nothing to do with it, that it belonged to one of his girls, but it was on his premises. On that basis the government took him to court. He was convicted. He appealed but lost on appeal. That was in 1977. I don't think he had very good lawyers.

Bernie was sentenced to serve three months at the federal prison in Lompoc, up the coast from Los Angeles. His penitentiary was one of the "country club" lower security variety, where they put white collar criminals.

"You know, as jails go, this is a country club," one of his lawyers said as he tried to console him.

"Yeah, counselor," Bernie shot back, "but as country clubs go, this is a jail."

At Lompoc they gave Bernie a job walking around holding one of those poles with a nail in the end, to pick up pieces of paper and other trash that had blown around the lawn. In his off hours he visited with the other inmates, people convicted of tax evasion, fraudulent accounting, and similar activities. When Ehrenfried and I went to see him, he told us they were all innocent. Everybody in the place was innocent. There were 400 inmates in the white-collar crime section. So he had 400 T-shirts made that said, "Free the Lompoc 400." They all knew that Bernie had them made.

The T-shirts didn't make Bernie very popular with the prison authorities. He wasn't too popular anyway because he made them put in a kosher kitchen at a cost of $75,000 or so. I don't know whether Bernie observed Jewish dietary laws before he went to Lompoc but he decided to once he was there.

The authorities probably concluded that it was cheaper to cater to Bernie than to try to fight him. They asked Bernie what time he wanted to leave on the day he was to be released. Prisoners could leave as early as 6 a.m., and Bernie said, "six o'clock." We were there to meet him, and so was the entire Lompoc prison population, to tell him goodbye.

• • •

Bernie spent a lot of his last years overseas because of his disputes with the SEC and the IRS. In later life he became something of a health food, vitamin, and diet fanatic. He couldn't cancel out all those earlier years of rich diets and lack of exercise. He died in London in 1995, at age 67. He was the most flamboyant man I ever knew, but also one of the most sympathetic and generous.

Chapter Eight

In Mexico: Condos, Timeshares, and Big Jugs of Lemonade

Let's return to the beginning of my first venture in Mexico. Later on you'll learn how my company gave a big tip to the president of Mexico. For now, remember that Lisa and I went to visit my friend Jess Kellogg in Cabo San Lucas, way down at the southern tip of Baja California. While we were there, Jess asked me to come down and join the Costamex sales team.

You know, when you leave one job or place for another there's always a push and a pull. The push was the awful weather in Toronto and the nerve wracking videogame business. The pull was the wonderful warmth in Cabo, the miles of wide, pristine, sandy beaches, the clear seawater, and the laid-back atmosphere. Recall that when we first visited, Cabo San Lucas wasn't much more than a fishing village with a permanent population of 910.

Cabo had still more to offer. While I was considering moving there a mutual friend of Jess's and mine warned me,

"You're going to need seven suits!"

"What are you talking about?" I asked.

The vacationers I'd seen down there were informal to say the least. If a woman donned a long blouse over her bikini she was practically formally dressed in those parts.

"Seven suits?" I asked him again.

"Yeah," he said with a little chuckle, "seven suits, all of them bathing."

The informality was great, but there was more. Ever since the Robo business I'd wanted to return to selling real estate. Here was a chance to get back into it, provided that my mastering of the laws, regulations, and local real estate codes of ethics wouldn't take too long.

"What does it take to become a real estate agent in Cabo?" I asked Jess.

"Simple," he replied, "just print up a bunch of cards with your name, address, phone number, and 'realtor' on them, and you're in business."

But there was still more. In the 1970s Mexico was moving into the late 20th century in a big way. In 1973 the government completed the transpeninsular highway all the way down Baja California. Before then you could drive to some parts of the Baja only if you had a Jeep, lots of spare time, lots of gas cans, and a desire to prove how tough you were. Otherwise, driving very far away from the towns wasn't feasible.

What that meant was that many places on the Baja were fly-in vacation spots for movie stars or the super rich who wanted to fish or just hang out. There was practically no commercial service, so most of the flying was done in small charter planes. But the transpeninsular was changing things for drivers. The airlines were beginning to look at service to places besides Mexico City, Guadalajara, and the other big cities. The cruise lines were beginning to look south along the Baja.

There were still more positives. Mexico was a very low-wage country by U.S. standards. Drinking water was available and inexpensive. Electricity, the same 60-cycle AC that we had, was reasonable. Real estate taxes were so low that the main bother about them was going to the local municipal building to pay them. Construction costs, again by U.S. standards, were rock-bottom. Anybody from anywhere could own a house or a condo. A foreigner couldn't own land in the coastal areas of the Baja, but he could hold land through a bank trust that was practically the same thing as ownership. He could sell, rent, lease, bequeath, or do anything else with his land that an owner could do.

Anyone who looked at the whole situation could see that, if they were willing to take a few risks and do some pioneering, the potential for cashing in on a big economic boom was there. At first I didn't analyze the picture that deeply though I was aware of the possibilities. What enchanted me at the beginning was that the Cabo market was a seller's market. Folks out fishing would see the building and when they got back to shore, would walk into the Hyatt Hotel where our offices were, and ask if there were condos for sale.

"Yes," I'd say and name the price. "Do you have the money to buy?"

"Yes."

"Fine. Let's look over the property."

That was about all there was to it. In fact it was so easy that I was hardly ever in my office. I had a sign on my office door, one side reading, "I'm at the pool." I'd put on one of those seven bathing suits and lie around the pool, working on my tan. As my tan developed I'd leave the pool earlier and earlier, and flip the sign on my door to the other side reading, "I'm in the bar."

The first Costamex development, Cabo Bello, in Cabo San Lucas.

The work – if you could call it that – was so easy I figured I must be leaving something out. Maybe I was doing something wrong that I'd be called on the carpet for sooner or later. After I'd been there about a week I asked Jess a question.

"When is my training program?"

"What training?"

"How do you do this? How do you sell correctly?"

"Come with me." he said, with obvious reluctance. We climbed to the second floor and went into one of the unsold condos.

"There's the living room, that's the bathroom, there's the bedrooms. But always remember this. People don't buy sticks and bricks."

"Come with me," said Jess, leading the way to the balcony. The balcony overlooked the smooth, sandy beach, the blue sea, and the gentle surf all lit up on one of those bright, clear days that the Cabo San Lucas Chamber of Commerce must have patented. We had this dialogue, with Jess speaking first.

"You see that big ball of light in the sky?"

"Yes."

"That's the sun."

"Aw, Jess, I know that's the sun."

"Now then, see those people frolicking on the sand? That's the beach."

"Come on, Jess, I know that's the beach."

"Those bathing suits the girls are wearing are called bikinis, and the drinks they're drinking are called margaritas. Sun, sand, beach, bikinis, and margaritas, that's what people buy, and don't you forget it. Oh, by the way, standing on that balcony next door, just last week, one of my owners told me that he and his wife were there, looking at the view with the full moon glistening over the ocean, and they held hands and renewed their wedding vows."

Well, Jess, I haven't forgotten: sun, sand, beach, bikinis, margaritas and romance. In fact, thirty years later I used the formula, except that my boss made me leave out any mention of bikinis in our brochure.

• • •

After we built out at Cabo San Lucas we went on to Acapulco, and from there to every other major resort in Mexico, including Puerto Vallarta, Mazatlán, Manzanillo, Ixtapa-Zihuatanejo, Cancun, and Cozumel. Every major city, too. They liked my work in Cabo so much they promoted me to national sales director, my shorthand title being project director.

Basically I did two things, trained and managed the sales force, and consulted with the development side of the company. The company, in other words, was split into two parts, the development and construction side and the marketing side. But the development people always called me in on design and layout matters because they wanted my opinion on whether or not a particular design or layout would sell.

We recruited our sales force mostly from the United States. Some Canadians joined us, and some women as well as men. We also hired some Mexican nationals who spoke English, because we knew that they could sell, and because we were, after all, a Mexican company. My training program was a variant of the "gate selling" method I've already described. In the first phase, establishing the need or desire, I told them about Jess's approach. I reminisced about us standing on that balcony in Cabo San Lucas, and Jess telling me that people don't buy sticks and bricks, they buy sun, sand, beach, bikinis, margaritas, wedding vows, and a whole lifestyle package. Over the years five hundred salespeople heard that story.

• • •

Acapulco was not just our first big development, it was the most exciting and challenging. That was because my boss persuaded the president of Mexico to give us the height limits we wanted. I had a role in smoothing things out that involves the president's wife as well as the president himself. You will remember at the beginning of this chapter that I didn't use the word "bribed" but called our transaction "giving a big tip." That's because a lot of people think of Mexico as a place where bribing rules, in contrast to the U.S.

There are reasons why we think that way, but the point I want to make here is that we dress up or disguise what really are bribes, whereas in Mexico they are more open about it. Remember that "consultantship" that Paul Meyer was asked to pay in order to create his own insurance company, the one that decided him against that line of work? That was a bribe.

The bribe Paul was asked to pay was really small potatoes. I'll digress for just a moment to give you three better examples about how bribing is systemic in U.S. politics. Do you remember California Congressman Randy "Duke" Cunningham? Probably not, because we tend to sweep bribery convictions like Cunningham's under the rug.

Cunningham went to federal prison in 2006 for accepting bribes from defense contractors. He admitted his guilt. He's trying to have his eight-year plus sentence suspended so he can be released. As of this writing he's still in the slammer.

Or take the example of Jack Abramoff, a bribing, corrupting lobbyist. He got four years in federal prison in 2008, even though his cooperating with the justice department resulted in the conviction of an Ohio congressman, an ex-deputy interior secretary, and several congressional aides. His friendly biographer claims that all Abramoff did was refine an already corrupt system!

The best example may be Illinois Governor Rod Blagojevich, who was accused in late 2008 of trying to sell the Senate seat vacated by president-elect Barack Obama. That was only one of a string of alleged corrupt practices, including handing out jobs and contracts in return for campaign contributions. The local U.S. Attorney on the case said, "We were in the middle of a corruption crime spree, and we wanted to stop it," as justification for tapping his phone and finally pulling the plug on Blagojevich by arresting him. The Associated Press story commented, "Blagojevich becomes the latest in a long line of Illinois governors engulfed in scandal." Blagojevich was so bad, even by Illinois standards, that the state senate removed him from office.

And we look down our noses at corrupt Mexico!

I could multiply the U.S. examples. The only real difference is one of attitude. We persist in thinking that bribery isn't part of our system and that almost everybody in business and politics is honest as the day is long. When a Cunningham, or Abramoff, or Blagojevich case surfaces, we dismiss them as aberrations.

Mexicans approach the matter more realistically. They soften their realism a little by using gentler language to describe the way the system works. The colloquial Mexican word for the bribe is *mordida,* but many folks prefer the word *propina,* or tip. They give a tip for doing one's job in a satisfactory way.

• • •

Let's start with my role in this and my catering to the president's wife. I had just bought a new Ford conversion van, a late 1970s or early 1980s model. This was in the early days of mass producing those vans using the bare-bones work van as a base. Mine had all the bells and whistles -- large windows, wood interior trim around the dash, doors, and windows, plus velour padding on the doors and headliners, four captain's chairs upholstered in leather, a wide bench seat in back, a stereo, a deluxe radio, a refrigerator, and a powerful air conditioner.

One day I was waiting at the Acapulco airport for clients, near the front entrance, when the president's wife stepped out of the terminal with her entourage. She always traveled with bodyguards, attorneys, secretaries, and other hangers-on. She was news wherever she went, so the press was there with cameras clicking and flashing. She was a large woman who stood out in the crowd, anyway. It was quite a show.

She spotted my van and commanded, "Stop! Wait a minute!"

She came up to me and my van and said, "What is this, it's really beautiful!" She spoke excellent English. I explained that they were made outside of San Francisco, got out of the van, opened the sliding door at the side, and invited her to look around.

"It's very comfortable as you can see," I said.

"Yes," she said, "it's a lot nicer than my Ford sedan. How do I get one?"

"Well, if you really like it, I can arrange for you to have one. I'll take care of it."

"Yes, I would like one."

"They come in black, red, and gray," I said. "What color do you want?"

"I'll take a gray one."

"OK," I told her. "I'll contact you when it's ready. I'll personally see that you have one of these vans."

First I went to the head of our marketing and told him that we were buying a conversion van for the president's wife. He was less than excited about the expense but I assured him that it would be a good investment. I was right. Then I went up to San Jose and placed the order, went back to get the finished van, and drove it into Mexico.

That was no big deal because I was in California on business from time to time. I called one of her attorneys when the van was ready. She really appreciated that van. From then on, wherever she flew, she sent the van ahead. It would be waiting for her when she emerged from the terminal. She loved riding around, sitting in back on one of those captain's chairs like it was a throne, behind those tinted windows, with her little refrigerator.

You have to know, in order to understand the next developments, that she and I became friends. She was so pleased with that van that she invited me to lunch whenever she was in Acapulco. We'd chat in a nice restaurant, with her entourage surrounding us. Now it was an open secret that her husband, the president, kept a mistress. The papers even ran a story alluding to the mistress, so the mistress matter was very much out in the open. One day I got up the nerve to ask her about her husband's other interest.

"I guess you're aware of the rumors."

"Oh, I know all about that," she replied. "To tell you the truth, I don't really mind, because I don't have to sleep with him any more."

I was a little startled that she'd say something so frank, but I think that having me to talk to in that way drew us closer together. The closeness would pay off later, as you'll see.

• • •

Meanwhile our company was struggling to get our building

permit for our construction project, where the tallest tower was twenty-seven stories. None of our other buildings were that tall but all of them were over the height limit of seven stories. Evidently somebody had told our company president, the developer, that there would be no difficulty because he wouldn't have authorized such tall buildings in the first place. Yet we didn't have the permits.

Functionaries from the state governor's office, the mayor's office, the building inspector's office, the port commission, the traffic engineer's office, all the people involved in the process, were pounding on my door every day, wanting to know where the permit from so-and-so was so that they could clear our project. Everybody had to agree so that we could get our building permit. We were at the point that the cement trucks were ready to pour. Still no building permit.

I kept calling my big boss, the developer, and he kept telling me, "No problem, no problem." One of the things you learn in Mexican society is that if somebody tells you "no problem," then you really do have a problem. It's on a par with someone telling you *"mañana." "Mañana"* doesn't necessarily mean tomorrow. All you know for sure is that it doesn't mean today.

Finally the developer called from Mexico City and told me, "O.K. I'm going to show you how things are done here. Come to Mexico City. Bring a suit and tie. I have an appointment with the president," meaning the president of Mexico.

I closed up the office and flew to Mexico City. I went into the developer's office to find two objects on his desk. One was a model of our proposed development, a precisely scaled miniature called a *maqueta* in Spanish. A clear plastic bubble covered it. The other was a rectangular block of wood with a locking doorknob in it. It was similar to the displays you see at Ace Hardware or Home Depot. A key on a chain was in the lock.

The developer handed the wooden rectangle to me and said, "You carry this. The chauffer is going to take the *maqueta*. We'll go in the car." We drove into lovely, wooded Chapultepec Park. Next thing I knew we're at the gates of Los Pinos, the Mexican White House. The chauffer stated our business to the guard at the gates. The gates swung open, and we rolled up to Los Pinos. We got out of the car, the chauffer carrying the *maqueta*. I held the wooden block with the doorknob and key. We were ushered into the president's office.

I should explain that the developer and the president were old friends. In fact, the developer was the godfather of one of the president's children. We were introduced all around. The president waved us into chairs so that we sat facing him across his large, polished desk. I was conscious of a restrained elegance in the room, with heavy drapes, the furniture sleek, generous, and comfortable, and thick carpeting. No Mexican kitsch here. The only jarring note for a foreigner unaccustomed to Mexico was a military guard with a sidearm standing behind the president. I was used to seeing armed guards in public places by then so all that registered with me was how odd the presence of an armed man in such a safe environment would seem to someone fresh from the United States.

The developer and the president began a conversation in rapid-fire Spanish. I didn't know much Spanish then but enough to know that what they were talking about had nothing to do with why we were there. It was about their families, mostly, but it was normal for the culture. Mexicans expected not to plunge right into the business at hand, rather they would spend a considerable time by our standards in discussing general topics. It was impolite to do otherwise.

Finally the president said, "O.K., what are you here for? How can I help you?" He knew darn well what we were there for but he shrewdly left the opening gambit to us.

"Well," the developer, my big boss, said, "as you know we are developing a project in Acapulco. We're going to be selling condos to the gringos. For dollars."

"Oh, good," the president said.

"And since they're condos, their owners will come back once or twice a year, and spend more dollars."

"Good, good," the president said.

"We have a small problem there, the seven-story height restrictions. They are preventing us from building what will bring in all those gringo dollars."

"Oh," said the president. Of course he already knew all about it and was waiting for the developer to state the problem.

The developer went on.

"You know, I was thinking of something very nice," and he pulled the *maqueta* over so the president could see one of the towers. He pointed to the top floor, "I think this would be very nice for your lady friend, whenever she's in Acapulco, to have a nice place."

"Yes, you're right."

My boss looked at me and said, "Give him the key."

I put the wooden block on my side of that big desk, the president looked at it, reached over and grabbed it, and slid it over to his side of the desk.

"Oh, thank you very much," he said.

Then the president got on the phone, calling the governor, the mayor, the building commissioner, everybody up and down the line, saying "We need to expedite this."

The developer suggested a meeting. The president looked at me.

"What's your name again, sonny?"

He spoke good English, like his wife. I was in my forties but to the president of Mexico I was "sonny."

"O.K.," he said into the phone, "I want you to meet Mr. Hickok at such-and-such a restaurant. Bring everybody you need to approve this, all your support people. He will have everybody he needs with him."

We had our meeting back in Acapulco the next day. Our engineer was there with a bag of cash, *propinas*, for everyone on the government side. The government guys sat down at the restaurant tables with their clearance papers and our blueprints. This was before the days of computerized plans so we had blueprints.

Now then, you don't have to be in Mexico very long before you know that everyone in any bureaucracy, public or private, has a rubber stamp. With their stamp seals on your piece of paper, you're in, or at least you can go to the next level of the bureaucracy. At that moment we didn't have one piece of stamped paper. We soon had many. Our guys were shoving the requests for permits at the government guys and the government guys were stamping them,

The Acapulco Plaza reveals its award-winning architecture. It was the first giant Costamex undertaking.

and initialing them without even reading them.

The government guys who were supposed to check our blueprints were doing the same thing. They began with the last blueprint in the stack, one hit on the stamp pad, one hit on the blueprint, flip to the next blueprint, one hit on the stamp pad, one hit on that blueprint, and so on. They never looked at the blueprints, except to stamp them. They could have been blueprints for a chicken coop or a rabbit hutch for all they cared. It was fun to watch. The chief building inspector and I sat in the restaurant and drank margaritas, looked on, and idled away the time until the paperwork was finished.

• • •

Well, I thought, that was that. How wrong! I got another chance to make lemonade out of a pretty sizeable lemon. It was a call from the president's wife. She didn't sound very happy, in contrast to her attitude on past occasions.

"I'm going to be in Acapulco tomorrow. We're going to have lunch. Meet me at 2:00!"

She named the restaurant. It was a command performance if ever there was one. For some reason, call it man's intuition, I brought along photographs of the model we showed to prospective presale buyers. It turned out to be a brainstorm.

I got to the restaurant on time. The president's wife and her entourage were already seated around a big table. There was one vacant chair next to her. She fixed me with a stare that could freeze the sun and pointed to the chair.

"Sit down," she commanded.

This time there wasn't any traditional Mexican preliminary bantering.

"I hear you gave *That Woman* a penthouse in your project." She almost snarled when she said "That Woman." She wasn't quite so blasé about her husband's mistress as she'd first suggested. I was mentally backpedaling in a hurry, then I thought of those photos I'd brought.

"Well, the company gave her a penthouse, you have to do things like that. But, let me show you something," I said as I showed her the photos.

I explained the layout.

"This building over here is where That Woman has her penthouse. It's all right, but its view of the bay is only so-so. We're not going to build any more penthouses in that building because of its location. Now," I said, "look at the taller building over here. It has a really nice penthouse. It has views of the sunset over the bay, is closer to the central-retail part of the development so you don't have to walk as far to the elevator. There's less landing and takeoff noise from the airport. It's the only one on the floor, so you'll have the only key to the floor. We can put a pool in there. You can have twenty four hour room service from the hotel, anything you need. It's much better than that other one. And I can let you have it for $300,000."

"I'll take it," she said.

My boss, the developer, was really pleased with my work.

I'd sold an expensive condo on a presale, and to the wife of the president, which gave us a good talking point to other buyers. The one he'd given away to the president cost us about $100,000 to build and was selling for $300,000. With a $300,000 sale I'd made back the $100,000 cost of the mistress's penthouse, plus a little profit on the sale to the president's wife.

My boss was so happy that he rewarded me with a larger than usual commission. I was so happy that I took Lisa and my Mexican girlfriend – my second marriage was over by then – to Paris for a weekend of shopping. We flew on the Concorde. It was an incredibly fast French-British supersonic jet that they later grounded because of its high fuel costs, and because people living near airports fussed about its noise.

My Mexican girlfriend, Andrea, and I at a reception at the Acapulco Plaza in 1979. Andrea's mother is at the lower right and as you can see, she is not too pleased with our relationship. My friendship with Andrea's mother blossomed after I bought her a house.

I reaped another reward from that sale. The restaurant staff saw me there with the president's wife on more than one occasion and made a note of it. I went back to that restaurant whenever I had a client I wanted to impress. They always gave me the red carpet treatment, the best table, the best service, and no reservations required.

• • •

I helped to make even more income for the company because I got us into timeshares. The economics were simple. If we built a condo for $100,000 and sold it for $200,000 then we grossed $100,000. If we built a condo for $100,000 and sold it to fifty people at an average price of $6,000 per week, then we grossed $300,000.

Of course the cost of rounding up fifty people was higher than selling to one, but the profit difference was still substantial. We only sold fifty weeks, keeping the other two per year for maintenance. I pointed out the economics to my bosses but they were unimpressed. The reason that they were unenthusiastic was that timeshares quickly became a racket. Not every timeshare enterprise was a racket, but enough of them were to give timesharing a bad name.

The reason that some timesharing became a racket was that initially it looked so great. Pay $6,000 and a yearly maintenance charge and you'll have a place to vacation for a week for, practically, the rest of your life. If you loved the location, say it was Acapulco, why go through the hassle of running around the globe staying at second rate places? Come back to this same place and get to know it over the years.

At first there was a craze for timeshares. The idea attracted people who wanted to get in on the ground floor of the latest thing, who wanted a guaranteed vacation in an exotic place, and who therefore weren't too careful about reading the fine print. There were absolutely no rules or regulations at first. It was a heaven-sent opportunity for scam artists.

The scammers had so many ways to set up their marks. One of the most popular was to greet the tourists at the airport with a ticket for a free breakfast at a nice hotel or restaurant, then harangue them for hours about these great timeshares. These guys were merciless. They'd play on the fact that some tourists were quite elderly, in their eighties, maybe with a touch of dementia, and they'd work them around to feeling obligated because of that breakfast. They'd sign up eighty-five year olds for thirty years of timesharing. They were good at lying. They'd say, "There are lots of timeshares. Oh, yes, you can swap timeshares. Sure, if you want to spend Christmas in Hawaii, no problem." The only thing they forgot to mention was that if you wanted to spend Christmas in Hawaii you'd have to be on the waiting list for five years.

There was one guy, even after we learned the business and laid down rules, who verbally abused potential customers. I'd fire him, he'd come back apologetic and contrite, I'd hire him back, and soon he'd be up to his old tricks again. Finally I had to let him go for good. Like any salesman, he knew that the wife made the final pocketbook decisions.

First he'd zero in on the husband, telling him how overworked he was, how much he needed a vacation, how wonderful the timeshare was, and all that. He knew that if he softened up the husband, he'd have an easier time with the wife. So he'd have John saying, "Yes, we can afford it. I need a vacation, the doctor told me to take a vacation every year," and so forth. So he gets down to Mary, the wife, and she says, "No. We can't afford it."

Then the salesman would go into his calculated rant.

"What do you mean you can't afford it? If you really loved poor, overworked John, you'd find a way to afford it! His doctor wants him to have a vacation but you don't! You don't even care if he ever gets a week's vacation, one lousy week a year to get away from his job! His job will kill him! You're probably one of those women, as soon as he croaks, you'll rip the ring off his finger, sell it, and take your mother on a vacation!"

Sometimes it worked. More often we'd have the poor woman, tears streaming down her face, running out of the sales office to complain to the manager.

Another racket the boys worked was to tell clients that prices were going up all the time and, "if you don't want to keep your timeshare after a few years, we'll sell it for you and you'll make money. It's a great investment!"

Unfortunately things usually didn't work out that way. Let's say a couple buys a timeshare and like almost fifty percent of U.S. marriages, theirs ends in divorce. Neither party wants the timeshare. If they bought it on the installment plan, they don't want the payments. They don't want to pay the annual maintenance fee. They don't want a place with memories of a marriage gone sour. So they put it on the market.

Or let's say a couple's marriage is fine, but they become bored with their vacation location, or suffer financial reverses, or an illness, or for whatever reason want to get out of their timeshare. So they put it on the market, too, along with all the others. There was a time, some years back, that a buyer could almost name any price for a used timeshare, and get it.

Here's a classic. My friend and boss at Lomas del Centenaro, Ed Rose, was selling timeshares and other real estate near Puerto Vallarta. Let me make it clear that Ed Rose is a straightforward, honest developer who warned his sales force about phony stories or exaggerations. Now then, a lot of beaches in and around Puerto Vallarta are rocky. They're nice to look at but not very good for lying out on beach towels or swimming from, except for folks who like cut feet. A customer came over to Puerto Vallarta from Cancun, where the beaches are wide and heaped with white sand. He asked one of the timeshare salesmen about the rocky beach.

"Oh, there's no problem," the salesman replied. "As a matter of fact, we're bringing in white sand from Cancun. Just a minute. Let me check."

He left the sales office and pretended to make a phone call. He came back.

"Yup, good news. They're already halfway through the Panama Canal! And if you sign up right now, we'll give you a free week in Puerto Vallarta during Christmas."

Yeah, sure. Just try to get Christmas week in Puerto Vallarta on short notice, free or any other way. Ed didn't know anything about this fraud until the client called him to make sure that he had that free week at Christmastime and "Oh, by the way, has the white sand from Cancun arrived yet?"

You might think those were all the scams that could be worked but there was at least one more. A developer would buy a piece of land, put up a sign reading, "Time Share," maybe clear the lot, even dig a hole, then put his sales force to work selling pre- construction units. The presales piled up. The developer said to himself, "Oh, gosh, I never had this much money before. I'm outa here!" And now he's living in Brazil enjoying his presale money. Similar scenes happened all over, not just in Mexico.

Scams like these led to changes in the law. For instance, presales now go into escrow accounts. Developers have to finish their buildings to withdraw the money.

Timeshare salesmen had a bad image: white shirt, white pants, white belt, white shoes, dark glasses, gold jewelry dangling from necks and wrists, and running noses from snorting cocaine around the corner when you weren't looking. They behaved in crazy ways, like getting drunk and driving cars into water fountains. Now there are laws about reading the fine print, and what you can tell a client. The laws haven't solved every problem but they have improved the image of timesharing.

Timesharing, done right, makes plenty of money. That's why I took a leave from Costamex and went to California to study the timesharing business from front to back. I returned with a plan that was legitimate and after a few tries got management to accept it. Now all the big hotel chains are into timesharing, although it's more often called fractional sharing or fraction shares. It's moved from selling just one week to larger blocks of time as vacations have become longer through the years. Also, "timesharing" had a poor reputation, so it was a positive advantage to find a new name.

• • •

The timeshare sales force I set up in the Acapulco Plaza led to one great example of how not to behave in Mexico. This story I call "Heinz and his birds."

To understand how this situation came about, you have to know a little background about the hotel business. We were developers and marketers, not hotel managers. So we turned over part of the management of the Acapulco Plaza to Holiday Inn. We kept some of the money makers for ourselves, including the gift shops, the eight restaurants, the condos, and the timeshares. We decided what proportion of the hotel complex would be for short-term guests, and what for condos. Holiday Inn had no say in that, so long as we had a reasonable number of hotel rooms for the Holiday Inn people to put in their reservation system.

The Holiday Inn folks brought in a manager named Heinz. Heinz was a German, tall, always clean shaven, impeccably dressed, and very fussy. He had a heavy accent. Looking at him, I often thought that if we could put a Nazi uniform on him, and a monocle in his eye, he'd be perfect for the role of an arrogant, overbearing German colonel in a bad World War II movie. He was used to German precision and top-down management. He didn't know anything about the way things were done in Mexico and he didn't care. His attitude was in sharp contrast to the one my training program instilled.

We taught our trainees that Mexico was a different mix of formality and informality, for example, you could wear informal clothing while selling in Acapulco, but if you were dealing with a Mexican, extreme politeness was a requirement. We also pointed out that in most cases the locals were on "Mexican time," that is "early in the morning" might mean 7 a.m. or 8 a.m. to the sales staff, but it could mean 10 a.m. or later to the local folks.

Well, Heinz was having none of that. He'd call staff meetings at 8 a.m. and nobody would show up. He'd go bananas, turn livid, rant and rave. Also, he didn't want timesharing in "his" hotel because he thought it gave the place a bad image. He'd come to me, demanding that one or another on our timeshare people be fired, despite the fact that it was none of his business who worked for us.

To keep the peace with Heinz, however, I'd fire them one day and hire them back the next. Heinz never seemed to notice. He'd shown me who was the boss and that's all that mattered to him. Everybody hated Heinz because he threw his weight around like that.

Now to Heinz and his birds. They were two large, beautiful

We developed resorts all over Mexico. This is the Cancun resort.

white birds, from China, I think. Heinz paid something like $20,000 apiece for them. Lord knows what they'd cost now. He kept them on long chains attached to perches, five or six feet off the ground, on the lower level of the hotel atrium. Their wings were clipped so they couldn't fly. They were part of Heinz's display down there, along with gardens, fountains and pools. Heinz was very proud of those birds.

On the next level of the atrium there was, among other things, a restaurant. One day two of the timeshare guys had a little too much to drink at the restaurant. While they were sitting at a table overlooking the lower level, one of them bet the other one that he couldn't hit one of Heinz's birds with a beer bottle. They had nothing against the birds, but they had a lot against Heinz. So the one guy threw the bottle, hit the bird, and knocked it off its perch. The bird landed on its back, feet in the air, dead as a doornail. The guy threw another bottle at the other bird with the same result.

I'm not condoning what happened to the birds, that's animal cruelty. I thought so then and think so now. But the attack on the birds was the only chance the salesmen had to get back at Heinz, and they took it. They wanted Heinz gone. Bad as their solution was, it worked.

Heinz saw the whole thing from his office above the restaurant floor. He came storming down, red as a beet, and ranted around, declaring that we were all worthless and beneath his dignity. I thought he'd have a stroke or a heart attack. After that episode he quit and went back to Germany. Holiday Inn replaced him with a much more reasonable manager.

• • •

As I've mentioned, after Acapulco we went around to all the resort areas and to the big cities, doing resorts and upscale hotels. After several years of working hard, learning a lot, growing a reputation as a master salesman and making lots of money, I thought I'd retire. I went to the Cayman Islands, south of Cuba, almost due south of the infamous Bay of Pigs. Did I retire for long? No. And, after a few years I wound up in Russia, of all places.

. The Holiday Inn resort in Puerto Vallarta. Costamex developed it next after the Acapulco Plaza.

Chapter Nine

To Russia but Forget About Love

My stay in Russia involved a horrible experience, some challenging times, and a few amusing incidents. I'll share some of them as we go along. First, though, I want to explain why I went to the Caymans and why I left. After that I'll relate the circumstances of my decision to go to Russia as well as those keeping me there and, eventually, forcing me to leave. The grisly event in Russia – the murder of a friend – hung over me for a long time but ended at last when my friend's murderer was himself killed. Then I could go back to a normal life without twinges of anxiety or fear. But let's begin with the Caymans.

When I went to the Caymans I was going to retire, relax, and ditch all my problems. I was going to rent a home on the beach in George Town, on Grand Cayman, and devote myself to windsurfing and snorkeling. I'd been to the Caymans on vacation once and that's what I did, windsurfing and paddling round in that beautiful clear water with my mask and snorkel, watching those brightly colored fish swim by. I thought it would be a great life, to be on vacation all the time. Why, I wouldn't read newspapers, watch TV, or worry about the state of the world. I'd read books on any subject other than how the world was faring. Oh, there were some people I knew there who were trying to get a resort underway. I was going to play a role in their business but it would be part time at most. The resort didn't pan out, and I was just as happy, because that left me free to do next to nothing.

Well, within three months of doing nothing except playing in the sun, windsurfing, snorkeling, and reading books, I was bored out of my skull. I was flying to Miami every other weekend just to get some action. I was frantic to do something meaningful and worthwhile. That's when an opportunity to buy a commercial real estate company came up. I bought it. The company's name was

My Cayman Islands company, Three Islands Real Estate, was located in this impressive building in George Town.

Three Islands Real Estate.

I did enjoy one other activity, teaching. Perhaps I'd sensed that retirement wouldn't be enough for me when I moved to the Caymans. For whatever reason I'd asked Cayman Immigration to put "instructor" on my work visa, a legitimate request because I'd taught real estate and other courses before. That notation on my work visa required me to do some teaching at the local junior college.

So I ran the real estate company and taught a real estate course. Having my own company and teaching were a lot better than goofing off but not entirely satisfactory either. That was because of the culture of the Cayman Islands.

The Caymans weren't the most diverting place on the planet

for me. The culture seemed a lot different than Mexico's. In Mexico the people aren't standoffish. If you learn a little Spanish and demonstrate that you respect their culture, they'll meet you halfway. They'll invite you into their homes, come to yours, and go sailing or fishing with you. When I lived in Mexico there wasn't a tight little expatriate community of gringos, sealed off from the rest of society. I expected the same kind of treatment in the Caymans, but didn't receive it. Locals in the Caymans were reserved and didn't appear to open themselves up to foreigners. After three years in George Town I was still as much a foreigner as I was on the day I arrived.

• • •

Then two things happened. A guy came along who wanted my real estate business more than I did, so I sold it to him. The second thing was, my friend Ehrenfried got in touch. He was my video game partner in Canada, who'd introduced me to Bernie Cornfeld. He'd moved on to an electronics distributing company in England and wanted me to come to Oxford, England to help him out. I went there happily, glad to work with an old partner, and glad to be out of the Caymans. I expected to be in Oxford for the indefinite future. What I didn't expect was that I'd soon be going to Russia.

My trip to Russia involved several circumstances. The first and most important happened in 1991 when the Soviet Union put itself out of business and split up into its constituent republics. The old Communist Soviet Union maintained the fiction that those republics had autonomy. Anybody with any sense knew they were part and parcel of the Soviet Union, the same Soviet dictatorship that challenged the United States for global leadership. Now the contest was over. The so-called Cold War between the Soviet Union and the U.S. disappeared so quickly that hardly anyone born after 1980 knows that it existed.

Russia was by far the largest and wealthiest of the new independent republics. It shifted from being a dictatorship to what it liked to call a democracy with blinding speed. The privatization of the Russian economy proceeded at the same rapid pace. Almost everybody in the United States thought that the transformation of Russia was a great thing because the Cold War was over, and we could reduce our military expenditures. The part about reducing our military turned out to be a pipe dream.

A lot of people imagined how wonderful the privatization was, with new oil multimillionaires in a country that a few years before allowed practically no private enterprise.

It was all well and good, but what people in the United States overlooked was how seriously the rapid change dislocated the old Soviet economy. Until a few years before the Soviet Union dissolved itself it was spending huge sums on military personnel, internal security and police, and especially on the armaments industry. It poured money into scientific research, applications related to arms and the military, and similar projects.

Almost overnight, a lot of those government people weren't needed. They were let go without any severance pay, or their salaries were drastically reduced. There wasn't a welfare system or unemployment insurance to ease them from one economic system to the other. Sure, there were fortunes being made, but many people were hurting.

This was when the "Russian Mafia" entered the picture. Their Mafia was different from ours, except for their being all business and playing for keeps. In its heyday our Mafia was regional, with boss families controlling the New York area, another group running Chicago, a third Miami, and so on. The Russian Mafia was organized on business lines, not regional lines. For example, the KGB, the Soviet secret police, ran the so-called rest centers, or resorts, for Communist bigwigs in the Soviet Union and all over the world. So naturally some ex-KGB people took over the operation of the same or similar facilities, for instance, the Moscow Country Club. More on the Moscow Country Club later.

Other groups took over cigarette sales, alcohol sales, car manufacturing, McDonald's hamburger restaurants, department stores, or whatever they were involved in before the Soviet Union collapsed. They created partnerships with U.S. people or other westerners because they needed capital and westerners had the money. Sometimes there were what you could call jurisdictional disputes over who got what, and there was rough stuff or shootouts just as there was in our Mafia. In other cases the Mafia wanted to muscle in on operations like those they already controlled, regardless of where the funding or capital came from.

Here's an example. I had a good friend who managed a hotel in downtown Moscow. The hotel Mafia wanted a part of his action. He refused and they kidnapped him, beat him up and dumped him in front of his hotel. That kind of thing happened a lot. It was like the wild, wooly West.

• • •

All this was going on when I went to Oxford. I didn't think much about it because I was wrapped up in the distribution business. Then I met a man named Bob Smith, which is not, by the way, his real name. In fact all the names connected with the Russian business are fictional. You'll see why. Bob introduced me to Olga, a beautiful young woman, petite, with blonde hair and blue eyes, the very picture of the Russian ideal. Her English was perfect. I couldn't detect any Russian accent at all. She was raised in Moscow but had gone to school in England and Chicago. She was, despite her polish and her looks, a tough cookie, a former KGB operative.

Naturally I was interested in what Olga had to say. She explained that there were really two jobs she wanted me to do. One was open and overt while the other was covert. Taking the overt or above-ground task first, it involved selling memberships in the Moscow Country Club and selling the dachas that the country club built or was building around the golf course. The Moscow Country Club wasn't just any country club. The famed industrialist, Armand Hammer, helped get it started and Bobby Jones, Jr. helped design the golf course.

When the old Soviet Union first opened up to the West, the idea was, westerners like to play golf, so let's have a nice place for them to play. The folks in the Soviet hierarchy thought that they might take up the game, too, just to pander to the West a bit.

Now for the covert side of things, a side that even Bob Smith didn't know about. Olga explained that a lot of former Soviet scientists were unemployed and that almost any promise to use their skills was tempting. These were the guys who'd developed the so-called "suitcase bombs," various small, highly portable nuclear devices easily concealed, at least at the time. The bombs were potentially devastating. Rogue states like North Korea were bidding for the scientists' services, with the help of another branch of the Russian Mafia.

Olga said that her people, former KGB people, were working with MI5, British counterintelligence and counterterrorism, and our CIA, to persuade these surplus scientists to retire. The idea was for them to have comfortable lives pursuing innocent activities in Russia. Maybe they would take up gardening or painting or novel writing.

It was hard to say no to Olga, who was way beyond cute and very persuasive, but I said no at first.

"I don't mind the sales part, in fact, I'm attracted to it. But the covert stuff, the political end of it, the intrigue, the potential for violence, I'm just not cut out for that," I said. Besides, I was in my late fifties.

"You've got to go for a younger guy. I'm not a James Bond type. I'm not up to this physically."

Olga knew how to get to me.

"Forget James Bond. We're not looking for that. We're looking for your negotiating skills with the scientists. And you'll have the perfect front, working in the Moscow Country Club. We have to have the best negotiator, and we know your skills. In negotiations, the best salesman wins. We know you're a really good salesman."

That did it. As I've said before, the highest compliment you can pay to me is to tell me I'm a good salesman. So she got me.

Little did I know what was involved in saying yes to Olga. She and her people wanted me to recruit other salesmen, some to do only the overt country club sales, a smaller group to use the overt work as a cover for the covert activity involved in getting those Russian scientists to see things our way. Those of us who were doing both the covert and overt work had to keep everything tightly compartmentalized. It was hard to recruit five people who

I knew could be trusted to go about their country club sales as though there were nothing else on their plates. They had to keep secrets even from their twenty fellow salesmen who were right at their elbows, working only on the country club side of things. I finally put together an overt-covert sales team of experienced men whose rectitude was unassailable. Or so I thought.

That was hard work but the training was even harder. Olga had promised no James Bond stuff but her colleagues didn't exempt me from James Bond-type, incredibly demanding, rigorous physical conditioning. For six months we began with three hours in the gym each morning, jogged for two hours, ate lunch, then went back to the gym for four hours more of exercise. I was way too old for this kind of exercise routine, and kept telling them that I had no business in a cloak-and-dagger operation. I'd promised Olga, so I stuck it out. But wait, there's more. They trained us in mountain climbing techniques. I could never understand why. Our handgun training was more practical, even if its implications were a little scary.

When we'd completed our training they issued us pistols and shoulder holsters. My Beretta wasn't a comforting going-away present for our trip to Russia. One thing stayed with me, though, and that was the importance of being in good physical shape because of its contribution to mental alertness as well as for physical well-being. I still go jogging every morning. Jogging helps clear out the cobwebs and get me ready for the business day.

• • •

On to Russia, and to the Moscow Country Club. Olga and others had shown me photographs of the place but I wasn't prepared for its nice layout and beautiful surroundings. The club's resort section was thoughtfully planned with large guest quarters. Each suite had a living room, bedroom, bathroom, and kitchenette. The common area included a spacious lobby, a nice bar, and a good restaurant. It was a first class deal. The course was a full, eighteen hole course, well planned. The club was just far enough out of town to be exclusive. It lay in a forest setting of tall deciduous

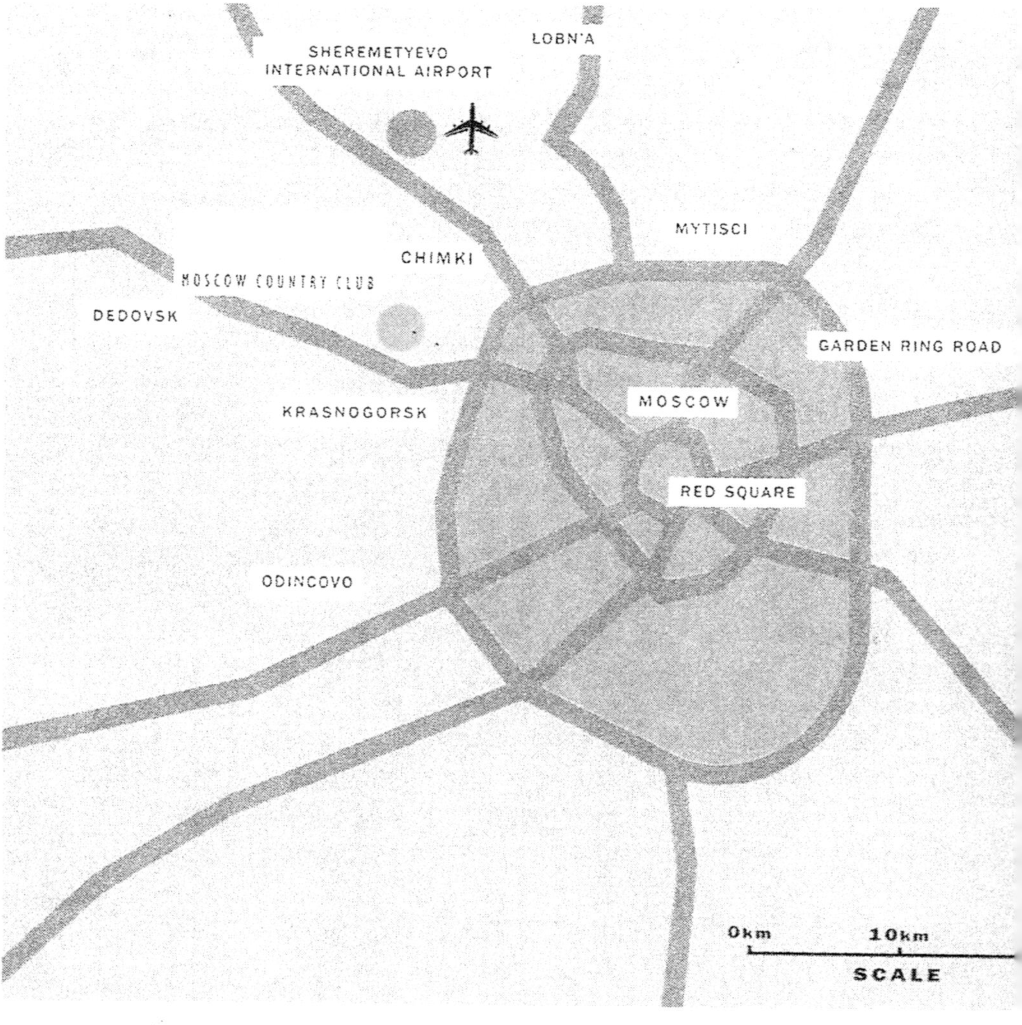

The Moscow Country Club, where my overt job was selling memberships and dachas. The country club was 30 minutes from the airport and was 40 minutes to Red Square. All maps and photos are from a Country Club brochure.

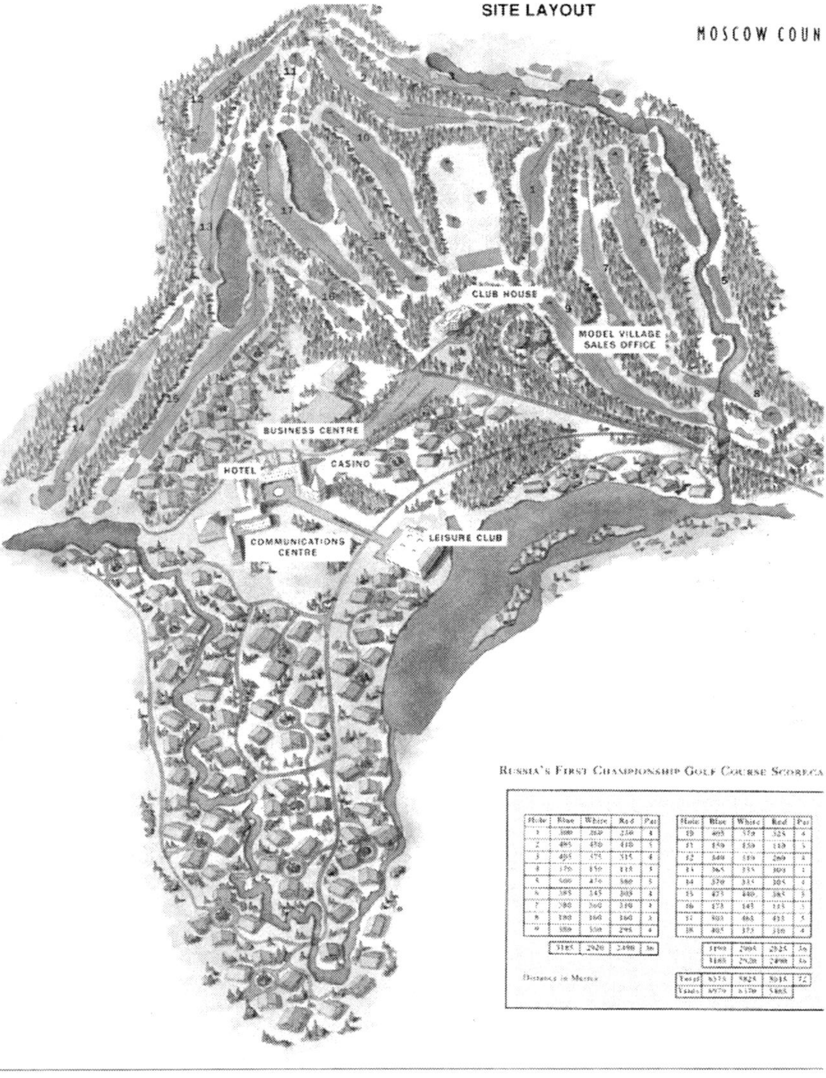

The layout of the Moscow Country Club, in a beautiful setting, just far enough from the city to make it an appealing destination.

trees, forty kilometers west and a little north of Red Square and nine kilometers from the ring road, a major artery. A members-only limo service took people from downtown.

Yet the project languished, with memberships going begging. Part of the problem was that the people under the Soviet system didn't know how to sell the club and its facilities. Another problem was the unsettled economic conditions, and a third was that the Russians, including those who had money, weren't into country clubbing and golfing.

Private houses, the dachas, were planned for the margins of the golf course. They were designed in a very attractive Craftsman-Stick Style that complemented their forest surroundings. Their sales were expected to help pay for the club's land and improvements.

A typical dacha. I owned one during my stay in Russia.

They came in four or five different designs, from a big 2,500 square foot model to a smaller villa at 1,200 square feet. The lumber was precut in Finland. Finnish crews came with the houses and assembled them on site. For all that, the dachas weren't selling any better than the memberships.

I was the director of marketing and sales. We already knew that our principal market would be the growing expatriate group in and around Moscow. We used proven sales techniques and they worked. To set an example I ordered a house for myself, and later sold it to the head of General Motors for Russia.

We did more than sell. We made the Moscow Country Club the place to be on Saturday night. We had concerts, sock hops, and country-western music in the big auditorium. We sponsored fashion shows, a boxing championship, Labor Day festivities, and a Fourth of July celebration.

One promotional scheme that didn't quite work out was the Finnish construction workers' idea to feature golfing in the snow. These were the guys who assembled the dachas. They were excellent workers but boy did they drink. They had to be drunk to do what they did after work, which was to go in to the sauna and get steamy hot, go outside where it was maybe thirty below, roll in the snow, then go back into the sauna. Anyway, they conceived the idea of painting the golf balls black so they would be visible in the snow.

I'd asked a CNN producer in Moscow to come out and do a story on us, and he got involved with our experiment. One of the Finnish guys went to a tee with a black ball and a club, hit a great shot down the fairway, and the ball disappeared into the snow. It was lost. Another Finn then constructed what he called a snow ledge that was supposed to raise the ball up out of the snow so that a player could hit his first fairway shot at the approximate location where his tee shot landed. It worked fine as a place from which to hit another ball but after the second ball landed, it too sank into the snow. One of the guys drew a circle with his mitten around where he thought the ball landed but he dug in the snow and couldn't find it.

It didn't help that the Finns were falling down drunk and that the rest of us were none too sober. I guess playing that way would

The interior of a large dacha.

have been OK for someone who didn't mind losing a golf ball with every shot. The CNN producer was filming all this as his feature on the Moscow Country Club. I had to bribe him to forget about it.

We had better luck solving another problem. Remember that many people were having a hard time surviving in the economic transition. The Moscow police were especially hard hit, so some of them went out on the highways and stopped expatriates, prime bait for hard-up cops, and extorted money from them under any pretext. They set up a guardhouse just outside our turnoff and hit up our members for cash. Here we were trying to sell memberships while the cops were holding up our members because they had the money, and our members were vowing not to return unless we did something about the cops.

I had a bright idea, a way out of our dilemma about the cops. I went to Olga and asked her to provide two "honeypot" girls who also used to be involved with the KGB. "Honeypot" was slang in the intelligence community for girls who would trade any sort of favors for information. Olga introduced me to the girls, Svetlana and Katya, from the "honeypot" sorority. I asked them to come out one Saturday afternoon.

Then I went to the bar, got a fifth of Scotch, and gave it to the girls. I told them to go to the guardhouse, give the cops the Scotch, have a nice party there, and stay as long as necessary to insure that the cops were warm and comfortable. Scotch was a pretty high-end treat for a Russian cop, not to mention Svetlana and Katya. I told the girls to tell the cops that they'd be back every Friday evening if the cops would stop hassling our members.

By Saturday night the cops could hardly stand up but they were navigating well enough to stop traffic. That is, they were stopping oncoming traffic so that our members could make a left turn onto the club property! They saluted our members as they drove by. What a successful turnaround, and what a good investment! The really great part of the story is that we sold all our memberships, with some Russians coming in at the end to see what this American fuss was all about. We hadn't quite sold all the dachas when I left. There were a few lots remaining but later those sold out, too.

Svetlana, a Russian honeypot girl, looking more demure than she really was, on a mission in Paris.

• • •

Now let's go on to the darker, grimmer, covert side of my Russian experience. Part of my job, you'll recall, was to convince those Russian scientists with suitcase bomb knowledge to stay at home and retire or semi-retire and devote themselves to peaceful pursuits. I never learned much Russian but Olga or one or two other young women, also ex-KGB, were always along to translate. My earnestness and main points came down well enough in translation that we conducted successful transactions with the scientists. MI5 and the CIA paid for all of it with money reaching us through private sources, mostly foundations in the U.S. Direct payment would have been bad form, of course.

It was Olga's job to set up an appointment with the scientists in advance. We'd always go to the appointments in one of those big, black twelve-cylinder Zil limousines. I wondered a little bit about the safety of those trips when Olga informed me that the Zils were armored and that the driver, and sometimes another guy up front, were also bodyguards. She mentioned that the guy driving the car that was always tailing us was a bodyguard, too.

I soon discovered that my worries were well founded. Once when we were headed to an appointment, an old car pulled up alongside of us, on my side of the big Zil. Our car was bulletproof, all right, but the back windows were down because Olga was smoking a cigarette. I looked out the window on my left to see somebody pointing a handgun at me. What happened next happened in much less time than it takes to tell.

I threw myself against the seat back of that big car, hoping to get the rear quarter panel of the Zil between my head and the business end of the handgun. At the same time I was trying to reach the little electric switch on the door to raise the bulletproof glass. With my other hand I was trying to get my Beretta out of its shoulder holster. The darn thing jammed in the holster. I'm thinking, "Here is my big moment, I'm supposed to use my handgun training here and I can't get the Beretta out, I'm not doing anything right, I'm too old for this, this is not selling real estate, what am I doing here?"

Meanwhile Olga took in the whole scene. At the moment of danger she was fishing around in her purse for her lighter. Instead she very calmly pulled out her big Glock pistol. She fired twice through my still-open window, Blam! Blam! She blew the windows out of that old car. Our driver/bodyguard floored the Zil and we roared away from the scene.

We thought it best not to hang around to see if anyone in the other car was hurt. The occupants of that car were our competitors who were trying to entice the scientists to go abroad to build suitcase bombs. At the very worst they were trying to kill us. At the very least they were trying to discourage us from keeping the appointment with a scientist they hoped to convert to their way of thinking.

The only casualty of the exchange was my right ear, so far as I know. Olga fired her Glock right next to that ear. You have no idea how loud a big pistol like that is in an enclosed space, even with open windows. I couldn't hear anything with that ear for some time. It was damaged enough for Olga and company to put me under a doctor's care, and I still can't hear as well with my right ear as with my left. The minor benefit for me from the encounter was that the doctor and I played tennis once it warmed up enough to go outside.

• • •

Another episode with Olga and her Glock was a lot more entertaining. This story unfolded at a Moscow disco, a vast building built for the Moscow Olympics several years before. The place was so big, it could hold 3 bands and 15,000 people without any one group's music, dancing, or drinking interfering with any anyone else. Olga liked to go to discos, so one evening we went to this cavernous building. There were a lot of Russian men and women there along with foreigners like me.

Now what I have to explain is the differing attitudes of post-Soviet women and men toward foreigners. In my judgment, the Russian women adapted to the new system much better than the men. Both genders were fed the same incessant ideological garp in school about the evils of capitalism, but the women accepted the new post-Soviet order of things. Their attitude was, "That was then, this is now, let's get on with it."

Not so the men. Whether they were more emotionally invested in the Soviet system, whether they had more difficulty adjusting to their new capitalist system, whether they resented more than the women their hoodwinking during the Soviet years, whether they wanted to take out their frustrations on representatives of somebody else's capitalism, or whether for some reason they just didn't like foreigners much, I can't say. I'm not a psychologist. I can only tell you the end result, which was that they sometimes made trouble in a place like this disco, where there was drinking and a less inhibited scene. The younger guys especially were tough to deal with. We were wandering around outside the joint when a big, burly guy deliberately bumped into me. Then he cocked his fists and in English said, "You dirty rotten blankety-blank, you don't bump me!"

Olga always did everything calmly. Very calmly, while lighting a cigarette, she stepped between us. She was, you'll recall, petite. He was big. She spoke to him in Russian. I couldn't understand what she was saying but I could tell by her gestures she was saying, "Calm down, relax, step back, we don't need this." She made some more comments. He smiled in response. She opened her purse and put her hand inside it, then invited him to look inside. He did, his smile froze, he turned to one side and took off like a rocket.

Later we sat down inside and were buying drinks.

"Olga, you'll have to tell me what that was all about. What went on out there?"

"Oh, I told him that he looked like a really nice young man, and that we could have a lot of fun together."

"That's when he smiled, but what was the business with the purse?" I asked.

"I invited him to have a look in my purse. I had my hand on my Glock. I simply told him that if he didn't leave us alone I'd have a good time blowing his balls off."

That was Olga.

• • •

My final Russian adventure was awful, and if you want to skip over it, I won't blame you. It happened that Olga and I were to meet a Russian scientist at a restaurant. One of my five covert salesmen, Mike, was to bring the scientist there. Mike was young, handsome, bright, and an excellent salesman. I'd known him in California and had flown from England to California to recruit him.

On the day of our meeting it was summertime, but pouring rain, raining so hard that Olga and I were late arriving at the restaurant. The restaurant was a sidewalk restaurant, part of a hotel but covered so that people could dine and look out on the street. There were some low bushes between the restaurant and the pedestrian part of the sidewalk, but otherwise there was a clear view between the street and the restaurant.

Our bodyguard wanted to go with us.

"No, don't worry," I said. "Just park the cars, we're only going into the restaurant."

We went up to the restaurant entrance and were waiting for the maitre d' to take us to Mike and the scientist, who were already seated. A moment later another car pulled up, braked suddenly, and Evan, one of my covert salesmen, jumped out. He dashed up to the low shrubbery, pointed a handgun at Mike, and shot him through the forehead. The exit wound blew out the back of Mike's head. Evan jumped back in the car as it sped away. There was pandemonium in the restaurant. Our bodyguards came running. The scientist freaked and ran away. I was totally distraught. I lost it. I wet my pants. I vomited all over myself. Olga, always calm Olga, was hanging on to me.

"I've got to get to Mike," I shouted.

"There's nothing you can do for him. We have to get out of here."

One bodyguard took one of my arms, Olga the other. They hauled me to the car, where Olga tried to clean me up.

I was berserk, completely out of control. They told me later that I was ranting and raving, gibbering unintelligibly and that I blacked out two or three times. I remember none of it. Olga had one of the primitive, many dollars-per-minute satellite phones of the era. She was on it, talking to her superiors, getting instructions from London. They told her to take me to our helicopter and get me out of Russia.

We had an old Sikorsky helicopter stashed in a barn out in the country. After some tense minutes Olga finally contacted the co-pilot. He came and flew me out of Russia to Finland. The rain was still coming down in buckets. The ceiling was so low that the co-pilot had to fly low, and for a while we seemed to be just a few yards above the Volga River.

After a week in Finland somebody flew me to New York, then to Miami, where I stayed in a safe house compound for a year.

I had to stay under cover because Evan had seen me watch him shoot Mike. The assumption was that Evan would kill me, too, if he could.

What had happened was that our Mafia competition had "turned" Evan. It was a shock to me because I'd trusted him, and regarded him as ideally suited for the job. But the Mafia knew of some weakness somewhere in his makeup or background and was able to blackmail him, or use the lure of money to turn him. It was my sad duty to phone Mike's parents and tell them about his death. Mike had a closed casket funeral. Meanwhile the CIA was looking for Evan. They contacted everybody, the Irish Republican Army, the Mossad, the Israeli intelligence service, or anybody else who might have a clue. Nobody'd seen Evan.

It was a long time before I returned to anything like normal. I had nightmares. I'd wake up in the middle of the night, sweating and screaming, replaying that devastating incident in the restaurant. Sometimes I still wake up at night, reliving that terrible moment.

• • •

Had I paid more attention to my intuitive daughter Lisa, Mike might be alive today. It so happened that shortly before the restaurant disaster, she and Scott, her fiancé and husband-to-be, were touring Europe. They knew I was in St. Petersburg and called to say that they would visit me. The last thing I needed was a family member involved in my double game.

"Wait," I said, "you can't come here. This is not good timing."

"We have our tickets and we're on our way," Lisa replied.

London threw a fit. They assigned bodyguards to Lisa and Scott wherever they went, even when we all returned to Moscow, even when they attended the Bolshoi Ballet. Lisa met Evan at a dinner party and said, "He's creepy. I don't trust him. Why do you work with him?" I should have listened. Both Lisa and Scott were asking all sorts of questions about what was this with bodyguards, and similar oddities. It was such a relief to see them out of Russia that I didn't really absorb Lisa's concern about Evan.

There were a few more loose ends to wrap up on this Russia

experience. Finally I was able to leave Miami, return to Seattle, find a consulting job, and start putting my life back together, as they say. Meanwhile, Lisa and Scott were going to be married in the Smith Tower, a magnificent old skyscraper at the south edge of downtown, then have a reception at my house in the suburb of Bellevue. It was all set, everything ordered. Then London called with the news that Evan was in New York.

"Get back under cover. Don't be seen in public."

"But the wedding, it's all arranged," I protested.

"Call it off."

So I did. Everybody was up in arms, all the wedding and reception guests, never mind Lisa and Scott. My pathetic evasion was that I was leaving town. Soon another call came to say that Evan had been eliminated. The story put out for public consumption was that Evan had run afoul of the Russian Mafia and was killed in a Mafia dispute, but I believe that the FBI shot him. The wedding was back on.

• • •

A year after the wedding my contract was up and I was able to divulge some things about the Russian adventure. I invited Lisa and Scott to brunch at the Red Lion Inn in Bellevue, and I filled them in as much as I could. Lisa was really upset. When I got to the Evan business she pounded the table and exclaimed, "I knew it. I knew about that dirty rat! I told you about him! I knew there was something fishy about this the whole time! We knew, we always knew something else was going on. We knew you weren't really selling golf club memberships. Why would you be in St. Petersburg selling memberships and houses in Moscow? And," she concluded, "if you ever do anything like this again, I'll kill you myself!"

Olga went on to another job under another cover in North Korea. For a time I got cryptic e-mails from her asking me to go cloak-and-dagger again. My reply was always, "I was too old for that stuff then, and I'm way too old for it now." Besides, I said, "If I do, Lisa has promised to kill me herself."

Still, someday, I'd like to go back, if only to find all my

belongings, including the brand new cowboy boots I left behind. When they put me on that helicopter for Finland all I had other than my soiled, filthy suit, was my passport. I still have friends there who are doing well and love Russia. Understandably, for several years I was in no mood to revisit Russia. I'd moved on to Thailand and to my current, second time around in beautiful La Paz, Mexico.

Chapter Ten

In Thailand and Mexico Again

When I went to Thailand I never expected to stay as long as I did, about six years, and I surely didn't expect to get married, but I did both. After the Russian adventure or misadventure I hesitated at first to commit to any long-term real estate development because the commitment has to be total, emotional as well as mental, if it is going to work. There can't be any holding back if I want my part in the project to go well. So I knocked around doing consulting jobs, which was work, but without the same kind of self-investment.

With consulting you give your employer the best advice you can, based on a thorough, objective study of his proposition in its financial, structural, environmental, and governmental contexts. The difference between consulting *on* a development and being *in* a development is this: at the end of the day, if you're consulting, it's still the developer's baby. If the other guy, the developer, takes all, part, or none of your advice, and you've given him your best advice, you're done. Whether he sinks or swims, you're out the door and on dry land.

Of course if you go around giving your best advice to projects that always sink, then your services won't be in demand. If they're all great successes, you'll be plenty busy. I stayed busy, but also thought about retirement. Neither option, consulting or retiring, or a third, being semi-retired and dabbling in real estate, held much appeal. As the Russian experience receded, I more and more missed the total immersion in a project that I'd enjoyed before.

• • •

Then the Marriott folks came along with an offer to help develop a resort in Thailand, on the island of Phuket. Phuket enjoys a beautiful setting off the west coast of the Malay Peninsula. It's just

I worked on several Thai developmen

'ing the Marriot Resort Hotel and spa.

far enough from the mainland to let the tourists feel that they're away from it all, yet it has an airport, wide, sandy beaches, and all the amenities. It's close to ideal for those Americans who are able to travel that far. My responsibilities for the Marriott Corporation were about the same as those for Costamex. Once we were finished on Phuket I went on to developments elsewhere in Thailand, finishing up in the town of Pattaya, southeast of Bangkok, right on the Bight of Bangkok.

I had a girlfriend in Pattaya. She worked in a restaurant, washing dishes and doing similar chores. I had a motorcycle, and she showed me all the fun places, hanging on to me as we roared around the streets and roads. She was young and liked to have new clothes and accessories, so I humored her and bought practically whatever she wanted. I was getting used to her, and we were doing fine, I thought. We had a standing arrangement to meet after she got off work. One day I was held up at my job and arrived late, to find that she'd gone off with someone else. There's loyalty for you.

I went into the bar, ordered a drink, and sat there pouting about how somebody had stolen my girl. Then I saw this other girl, a really pretty girl, dancing with another girl. I asked the pretty girl to dance. She spoke no English then and I knew only a little Thai, but I got the idea across and we danced. We hit it off despite the language barrier. She was from Bangkok, on vacation to visit her cousin, who was the girl she was dancing with.

• • •

I took my new girl around to all the places my ex-girlfriend had shown me, and we went out every night. I began teaching her English. Nat – her full name is Nathakan – is extremely intelligent, and a quick study with a gift for learning languages. When she wanted to compliment me on teaching her English or, in fact, anything else, she'd call me "My teacher." She'd say, "You are my teacher." I convinced her to extend her vacation.

Eventually Nat had to return to Bangkok because she had a business there, a clothing factory making garments for the Tommy Bahama line. She was not just supersmart, but an excellent businesswoman. In addition to all those positive abilities, she was a first-rate cook who fed us gourmet meals every evening. She'd worked in a first class restaurant while attending designer school in Bangkok so she knew everything there was to know about Thai cooking and food. Nat was everything a man could wish for, except for the fact that she was in her twenties and I was in my sixties. I had doubts about a long-term relationship. I told her, "You need to find a young man, not an old goat like me."

Now if you're an older man reading about my hooking up with a twenty-something you're probably thinking, "Where's the beef?" or "Some guys get all the breaks," or "This guy's got a talented young woman on the string and he thinks there's a problem?" Well, I thought there was a problem and I'll tell you why. So far as my observation went these May-September marriages rarely worked out. After almost four decades of bachelorhood I wasn't sure I wanted to marry again. Then there was the issue of citizenship and residence: her factory and all of her family were in Thailand, while all of my family and most of my business contacts were in the United States. I continued to tell her, "I'm way too old, you ought to find a young guy."

Soon after she returned to Bangkok I had to spend some time there, so I stayed with her in her nice penthouse apartment and we continued our talk. One of the things that attracted her to me was that I was a *farang*, a foreigner. If this seems odd, let me explain how the world shapes up for a Thai girl.

If a Thai girl wants to marry she has, basically, one of two choices. She can marry a lad from her village and settle down to a life of having babies, raising kids, doing chores, and living the village life, a life that's less than thrilling. Or she can do what Nat did, get out of the village, go to the city or at least to one of the big towns, and start trolling for a husband among the ambitious young men with good futures. When she does that, she runs up against another problem, different from the one facing the girl who stays behind, but maybe just as serious.

As the Thai girl's bright and ambitious young husband becomes prosperous, he often takes another wife, and then another and maybe still another. He may set up separate housing for the added

Nat.

My office after completing it on property that my wife Nathakan "Nat" and I purchased in her home town near Udon Thani, Thailand.

wives or he may bring them all home to live under the same roof. The practice has nothing to do with Islam or any other religion, it's just the culture. Here's where we *farangs* are especially attractive to Thai girls, because we, supposedly, marry only one person at a time.

Anyway, we kept on talking about our relationship, and in the meanwhile time went by. After about a year I'm thinking that this is a nice program, a good, comfortable life. The one thing I didn't want to do was embarrass my children over this situation by bringing Nat to the U.S. and announce that she was my new wife. I could hear them telling one another, "What's he doing with this kid who's younger than we are?" And "There's no fool like and old fool!" And "We thought he'd come to his senses after that Russian mess but here he's gone off the deep end again," and "yadda, yadda, yadda."

Besides, I wanted to see my new grandson, Lisa's baby. I especially wanted Lisa to meet Nat and have her impression of my sweetheart before doing anything rash. At the time Lisa was thirty-nine and Nat was twenty-nine, and I thought that even their age difference could be a barrier. But Nat and Lisa got along really well, right from the beginning. In fact, Lisa was so happy with Nat that she arranged everything for the wedding and reception. We had both at her house. So we got married and returned to Thailand, to Nat's home village, near Udon Thani in the northeastern part of the country.

• • •

I decided to retire and concentrate on leading a laid-back life in the village. Nat owned property there and I added more acreage. We built a beautiful house out of mahogany and teak, all of it; exterior, interior, walls and floors. It's illegal to cut most trees in Thailand, so you have to find deadfalls that haven't been harvested by somebody else, or find a teardown and use the lumber from it in a new house. We bought three houses and had them demolished so that we could build what we wanted. Downstairs we had a great room for family gatherings and an elaborate kitchen for Nat when she wanted to cook. Upstairs was our private domain, a master bedroom with a lovely view of mountains, the river, a lake, and rice fields, our fields and others'. It was just about perfect. Nat found that she could stay in touch with her factory by phone, e-mail and occasional flying visits.

I enjoyed watching the round of village activities. The farmers, most of them, lived in the village, along the main street. Their farms were a few miles out. They and their families went to their farms on motorbikes and would stay for a week or so at a time in huts elevated above the flooded rice paddies. They'd be planting, harvesting, or irrigating, or just waiting for the rice to grow or sometimes, the rain to come. Then they'd return to the village after

I'm in the front row, right, with my wife's nieces' English class. This is one of their frequent Saturday morning visits to our house to practice their English.

they'd finished whatever they were doing on the farm. Most of the time the local stores met our needs but we lived close enough to an airport that we could go wherever we wished for more extensive shopping.

My unique pet, a water buffalo, was a kind of fillip for the Thai scene. After we married and returned to Thailand, Nat got me the baby water buffalo for my birthday. He was tiny, as water buffalo go. His mother died giving birth to him, so at first I fed him with a baby bottle. I named him Buffy. We bonded. Our bonding was most unusual, because in Thailand water buffalo aren't pets, they're work animals. They're tractors. Even the people who own them and care for them aren't around them much because they have an attitude and b-i-i-i-g horns.

But Buffy was different because he wasn't raised to work, like other water buffalo, but to be a pet. As soon as he was big enough, I started riding on his back and teaching him English. He caught on quickly, and soon he knew "stop," "back up," "turn right," "turn left," and "go forward." We had another pet, a cat named Mew Mew. The three of us were quite a phenomenon in the village.

Almost every day that I was home I'd pick up Mew Mew, put her on Buffy's head, get on his back, and we'd go right down the

Here's Buffy, my pet water buffalo. He looks formidable, but is really a gentle, playful animal. I raised him from infancy, then taught him commands in English when he grew old enough to ride.

main street of town. Sometimes we were about the only traffic on the street, which was just a dirt street with, mostly, one-story houses on either side. All the kids would come out, laughing, running around us, and following us, Mew Mew on Buffy's head, and I on Buffy's back, wearing my swim trunks.

The main street led down to the river. You wouldn't confuse the local river with the Mississippi but it was wide enough to irrigate the land around and more than deep enough to swim in. It didn't contain all the nasty stuff that too many people in the West associate with Asian rivers. We'd go right down to the river's edge. I'd put Mew Mew in a tree, then Buffy and I would jump in the water, swim around and splash each other. Buffy loved the water, and he loved to dunk me. When we tired of our games, I'd pick Mew Mew out of the tree, put her on Buffy's head, climb aboard Buffy's back, and we'd plod back home. Our return trip was just as much fun for the kids as our trip to the river.

• • •

Yet for all the relaxation of the retirement life, and for all the fun of being married to Nat, something was missing or lacking. I guess my first clue should have been getting busy with our collaboration on designing a canvas top for pickup trucks. She had them made in her factory. The canvas top wasn't as durable as a metal topper but it weighed a lot less and was easier to store. If you've ever wrestled a regular topper off a truck and then looked around for somewhere to put it, you know what I'm talking about. We sold some canvas tops in Thailand, and were looking into exporting them to the U.S. Some retirement! By then, though, I'd decided to return to the U.S., at least for a while. But Nat wanted to stay with her business and in any case was a long way from being retired.

The too-easy life wasn't the only thing pulling me away from Thailand. My kids and grandkids were giving me a hard time, saying things like "You're never coming home," and "You've abandoned your family." So I returned to California, then went back to Mexico, which is a lot closer than Thailand to my kids, grandkids, and great-grandkids. As it turned out I once again got to know the point of the old joke, "My wife's a great housekeeper. When I left my wife kept the house!" Not that we've split. Our marriage is still a work in progress, and it may be that she can visit me here, now that I'm settled in again. Or, as soon as my life slows down a bit, I can visit there, even go back and forth. She may dispose of her business. As I say, it's all up in the air right now.

We do stay in touch by phone, which is all right but doesn't always produce the best results, mostly because I sometimes try to be smart. Not long ago, for instance, she called in what for me was the middle of the night. She was on the other side of the international date line and it probably was broad daylight for her, so she didn't think about what time it would be in Mexico's Baja. When the phone rang I put it up to my right ear, the one that Olga's Glock had damaged years before, and sure enough I heard only faint sounds.

"Who is this?"

"It's your wife!"

I could have said something like, "Oh excuse me, it's my mistake, darling. I'd dozed off and am a little groggy, that's why I didn't recognize your dear, sweet voice." But I didn't. That's when I made my second mistake. I thought I'd be clever and change the subject, so I said:

"How's Buffy?" Not smart.

"You care more about that damn water buffalo than you do for me! All he does is eat."

There wasn't any way that anybody could get Buffy to do a lick of work now that he had grown up as a pet. It was hard to get our conversation back on track after that, but I was happy to learn that Buffy was still down on our farm, even if he was eating a lot. I hope he misses me.

• • •

When I went back to California I landed another consulting job, this time for a headhunting firm, but consulting was no more satisfactory in the long run than it had been in the past. Fortunately I soon got a call from my old friend Ehrenfried Liebich, my partner in the video game business who'd introduced me to Bernie Cornfeld. Ehrenfried founded a company called Eurectec to recycle tires. He saw that old tires were potentially valuable resources but meanwhile they were creating a monumental environmental hazard because they absorbed a huge volume of space in waste dumps.

Worse, they often blazed up from the underground fires that burned in municipal garbage dumps. When they burned, they sent up a great billowing cloud of oily black smoke that settled on cars, houses, grass, trees, gardens, and people. The fires were nearly impossible to put out. The stench was terrible.

The public was tired — no pun intended — of the environmental damage and was putting the pressure on governments to do something. In case you think I'm exaggerating this problem, Ehrenfried estimated in the early 1990s that a staggering 275,000,000 and more tires were dumped every year, just in the United States and Canada.

By the time I came on board Ehrenfried had perfected his organization and had developed the best tire shredding machine in the business, the Compact 6000 Granulator. This wonder manufactured so-called "crumb rubber" in several different sizes for various applications. Crumb rubber's most common use was an asphalt additive for streets and highways. The crumb rubber mix was smoother, quieter, and when properly mixed, more durable than ordinary asphalt or, for that matter, concrete. It works fine in all kinds of weather.

The highway contractors hated us. They wanted concrete roads, noisier, more expensive, and costlier to maintain. The federal Intermodal Surface Transportation Efficiency Act of 1991 mandated crumb rubber additions and the highway contractors were furious. Among other things, they said that our highway material would catch on fire. Never happened. How matters played out is not part of my story but the upshot is that now practically every state mandates crumb rubber additive.

Besides granulation, a Eurectec client could buy an entire plant that took whole tires in at the back door, separated the steel belting and rubber, and sent different sizes of crumb rubber out the front door. There were many uses for crumb rubber. We replaced a lot of running tracks at schools.

One great use is for playgrounds because it's safer. When kids hang upside down and lose their grip, or miss a handhold on the monkey bars, they land on three inches of rubber. The old playgrounds were made of rocks, sawdust, cinders, or hard compressed earth. Ouch! Crumb rubber sidewalks were easier to walk on and didn't crack like concrete when the tree roots forced them up. Kids on bikes rode over a bump instead of taking a header into a crack.

I bought into the company and took charge of sales. Back then ads in the print media still paid off in a big way. We advertised in the *Wall Street Journal, USA Today,* and especially *Entrepreneur Magazine* as well as other outlets. Factory people came to us when they had all the other equipment but wanted a first rate granulator. We also had a press that converted crumb rubber into outdoor products like roofing tiles, speed bumps, traffic cones, and sound barriers. Indoor products included fatigue mats, floor mats, and carpet underlays. As I said, in addition we could, and did, set up an entire factory, back door to front door, on a turnkey basis.

I sold all those types of operations, the granulator, the press, the entire factory. I could show them a granulator's operation because we made a deal with a nearby California state prison to have one there, with prisoners running it. I got involved in product sales, too. It was challenging and fun, for a while. But then California, especially our location in the Los Angeles area, began to wear on me. I couldn't find a residential subdivision to live in that was really comfortable, away from the crowded freeways, the noise, and the press of people. Luckily, another old friend Don Rockwell, "Rocky," called. We'd worked together in Mexico years before. He'd seen an article in the San Diego newspaper about an Ed Rose who was beginning a project near La Paz in the state of Baja California Sur. We agreed that this had to be the same Ed Rose we'd known years ago.

• • •

I knew Ed from personal acquaintance but also by reputation, because he had successfully established residential projects, golf courses, and developments in other Mexican resort areas. He'd decided to semi-retire. He'd gone to La Paz, opened a bed and breakfast on the Malecón, the waterfront boulevard and walkway. Then he began a residential development in El Centenario, on the transpeninsular highway a few miles outside of La Paz.

So I called Ed just after he'd begun the Lomas del Centenaro project. You'll recall that it's the project I used to illustrate the "gate selling" method, framing my discussion in the past tense because we're almost sold out now.

I asked Ed if he remembered me and he said he did.

"I'm bored to death with California, I hate the traffic, I'm sick and tired of the whole thing, and I want to come back to La Paz," I told him. Then I asked him, in words Lisa once used to describe me, "Have you got anything for a high-mileage unit in good working condition?" And he said, "Sure, I actually do and I'm going to be up in your area in the next few weeks. Let's meet and we'll talk about it." We did, and I came down here beginning in March 2003.

So I'm back in the La Paz area. The area is wonderful for two reasons. The first is, I'm a member of the sales team at Lomas del Centenario company, the crown jewel of a pre-eminent developer at the summit of his career. The second reason is, this area is the most comfortable one I've ever been in. When my youngest daughter asked, "Dad, why are you here, when you could live anywhere," I replied, "because it's comfortable." I'm comfortable with the climate that has benefited my arthritis, with the people, the economy, and the multiple attractions of La Paz and its vicinity.

Let me explain. You'll remember that in the early 1970s I was pioneering real estate sales in Mexico at Cabo San Lucas. Cabo, as the in-crowd likes to call it now, was nothing like it is today. Then it was a fishing village with a small airfield, a few dusty streets, and narrow roads that connected only to other lower Baja communities. A tiny grocery, little more than a shack beside the owner's house, sold odds and ends of fresh and canned food. You could exist on its wares but not really live. There was nothing, but nothing, going on in Cabo San Lucas outside of our own development. When the sun went down, day life ended. There wasn't any night life. In other words, Cabo was a great place for commercial and sport fishing but not much else.

That's why my coworkers and I went to La Paz, then and now the major city in the lower Baja region. We went there for government contacts, legal advice and assistance, and for practically everything else including shopping, good restaurant meals, entertainment, all car repairs beyond the ability of a shade tree mechanic, and medical and dental care. I left the lower Baja region after a while, but never forgot the appeal of welcoming, diverse La Paz.

When I heard of a chance to return to the La Paz area I jumped at it. Of course La Paz has changed since the 1970s but almost entirely for the better. It is the capital of the state of Baja California Sur, and has all of the services you would expect in a contemporary government center. Club and cafe entertainment is there if you want it. The food is great, whether you are eating out or buying in the public markets or the supermarkets. There is a settled United States and Canadian population large enough that one restaurant features a "gringo night" every Wednesday, complete with a band and female vocalist. Another restaurant offers two band nights, standards and old favorites on Wednesday, country and western and classic rock on Saturdays. The band has two vocalists.

A Wal-Mart and Sam's Club, an Office Depot and an Office Max are among a variety of supermarkets and specialty stores. The Home Depot is the largest hardware emporium. A sixteen-screen theater shows American movies with Spanish subtitles. The Malecón, the walkway along the bay, is enchanting at any time of the day or night.

With all that, La Paz is not a tourist trap. Oh, there is tourism but it hasn't taken over this city of 200,000 the way it has Cabo San Lucas and San Jose del Cabo, with their pricey high-rise hotels, traffic jams, noise, and sharp characters looking to make a few extra pesos off naïve tourists. Instead, La Paz is as welcoming and friendly as ever, with first rate hospitals, beaches, satellite TV, and all other communications services. La Paz means "the peace," and the people really mean it. The crime rate is low, so low that I feel as safe or safer on the street or in my house than I did in the United

States or Canada, and safer, for sure, than in post-Communist Russia. The police are there to enforce the law and to help, not to hassle tourists.

I mentioned the climate. It's warm much of the year, averaging about 75 or 80 degrees Farenheit. Sure, it's hot in La Paz as it is in most of the Baja at times, but it's generally milder than it is in Cabo, the artist colony of Todos Santos, or many other settlements. The weather's better too. Islands and mountains dampen the effects of hurricanes.

More than all this, La Paz has a real economy. As the state capital, it employs thousands. Tourism is important, but it isn't all that's going on. La Paz is a major transportation center. The airport features direct or connecting flights to anyplace in Mexico or the rest of the world. The transpeninsular highway is an easy drive to the United States. Ferry services sail to the mainland via Topolobampo and also to Mazatlán, which is better known to most people in the United States. Pemex, the government oil monopoly, runs a large refinery. The power plant feeds many communities in Baja California Sur. Fishing is a major commercial activity as well as a tourist draw. Truck farming is largely hidden from the view of casual visitors but it is also an important part of the local economy.

OK, perhaps all this reads to you like a chamber of commerce brochure. But I wouldn't write any of it if I didn't believe all of it. I've worked in different places in the United States, besides living, working, and vacationing all over the world. I've visited many other places. Been there, done that. After all of it I am where I want to be, in La Paz, Baja California Sur, Mexico.

• • •

Now let's move on to my company, Lomas del Centenario. Lomas is no vest-pocket development. It's a rectangle of about seventy acres stretching up a hill in El Centenario, a pleasant town ten minutes outside La Paz. Lomas' developer chose the site because of its panoramic views of the city, the hills and mountains, and the Bay of La Paz. He provided electricity, water, sewers, and concrete sidewalks. The lots are a generous one quarter to one half

A small segment of the Malecon, the bayside street in La Paz. The Malecon runs for con a favorite place for tourists and townspeople to stroll or just relax.

iles around the bay of La Paz. Inviting beaches and palapa umbrellas make the Male-
Jon Lehr photo

an acre. We've sold most of them, of which I've sold the majority including one that I bought myself. There are some seventy homes built, under construction, or planned.

Lomas del Centenario architects create graceful interiors, utilizing space to the utmost and attending strictly to detail. The developer is thorough, careful, and double-checks everything. The development is in a desert but it's a lush desert, filled with cacti and native trees such as the tall, spreading palo blanco. Introduced trees do well, including flowering almonds and eucalyptus. If you've spent any time in office building atriums in the United States, you know the ficus as a kind of gangly potted ornamental. Not so here. The ficus trees that we have in the outdoors provide beauty and shade with their graceful white branches and glossy green leaves.

Am I shilling for my company? No, I'm not. My over fifty years' selling experience tells me that if I can't honestly admire my company and approve of its work, then I'd better find another job. The strain of defending a dishonest or slipshod organization isn't worth it.

• • •

As long as we're on the subject of Mexico, let me dispel three time-worn myths about this country. The first is that Mexico is a dangerous place. I've remarked on that briefly, but let me address this myth directly. Mexico is dangerous, because if you aren't careful, you may get a sunburn! The online and print magazines, the bloggers, and the newspapers, even the U.S. state department, get a lot of mileage from their warnings about Mexico. Sometimes they don't pinpoint locations or they generalize about large areas.

The assumption back of these blatant exaggerations is that if you just stay in the good old U.S.A. you'll be fine. The truth is, there are lots of places in the U.S. that no prudent person would go alone, or after dark, or even in a group at almost any time. Most places in Mexico are safe. Even more places are safe if you keep your wits about you and don't go looking for trouble. Mexico is no different regarding safety than the United States or most other countries I've been in, and it's a lot safer than some. And, to repeat,

La Paz is one of the safest cities.

The second myth is that real estate is an uncertain investment in Mexico. This is nonsense. U.S. citizens or anybody else can buy property outright if the property is far enough away from a border or a coastline. In a place like the La Paz area near a beautiful bay, a foreigner holds property through a bank trust giving him or her all the rights of ownership. Of course, you have to deal with reputable firms and examine carefully what you are signing. People who haven't have lost their investments. But don't tell me that everybody who buys property in the United States is able to keep it, either.

The Mexican government isn't about to stop encouraging real estate buying because it knows that tourism and other foreign investment is an income producer second only to petroleum. Unlike oil, it's renewable. Mexicans call tourism their "smokeless industry." In fact the Mexican government is so anxious to promote real estate investment that it imposes no inheritance taxes!

The third myth, related to the first two, is that Mexico is a sort of banana republic where wobbly governments come and go, and temperamental politicians alter fundamental policies on a whim. This is a complete misconception. The media get a lot of traction from overreporting events like the aftermath of the 2006 elections. Then the loser in the presidential race fussed and fumed and ranted about it, while his supporters took over the main square in Mexico City. The government prudently did nothing to dislodge them. An independent commission affirmed the fairness of the election, and the squatters in the square eventually went back to their homes and jobs. By then the media had gotten all it could out of what basically was a non-event and moved on.

Meanwhile, some intelligent and thoughtful people in the U.S. were convinced that all of Mexico was in an uproar and that revolution was imminent. When it comes to Mexico, the U.S. media aren't concerned with cultivating public understanding. Instead they cater to a belief that Mexico is full of volatile Latins who are at each other's throats whenever they aren't taking a siesta. They would like us to think that any Mexican government is transient and ineffective. This is a shallow misinterpretation of the worst kind.

• • •

Mexico enjoys a high level of environmental awareness and imposes strict rules about any development. You don't just go out and whip together a subdivision or throw up a hotel. You tell people that, and if they have the media - cultivated image of Mexico as full of bandidos and crooks, they ask you, "What have you been smoking?" But, like the beauties and conveniences of La Paz, it's true.

If you're going to build a development in Mexico you have to have a detailed topographic survey, arrange for sewage treatment or septic tanks, have a street and traffic plan, and have a big building like a hotel sited on your maps. You can't commandeer a beach because in Mexico all beaches are public. You must provide access to a beach and you must not encroach on it without a permit. It is possible to build on a beach but the permitting process is so involved and expensive it usually isn't worth it. Even then, you cannot block the beach completely.

The list goes on. If you are building in a protected area, and almost all buildable areas are protected to some degree, you can't plant any old tree or shrub. If you are building in a designated natural area you can use only native plants. That's partly why Lomas del Centenario is so elaborately laid out.

Parts of Lomas del Centenario are in a protected zone, controlled by a federal overlay limiting the kinds of plants allowed there. Some residents in that area thought it would be nice to plant bougainvillea around their houses, but federal environmental agents spotted the bougainvillea and made them remove it. Why? Because bougainvillea isn't native to that area.

Everybody knows about the restrictions. The residents reasoned that the Mexican government wouldn't enforce its own regulations. They were wrong, but they weren't hurting after they lost their bougainvilleas. There are plenty of beautiful, available native trees and shrubs that grow well and bloom in sequence all year round.

When Ed's project sells out, I'm thinking of retiring again. Will retirement stick this time? Who knows?

• • •

Now, with that said, you have my life before you: the car selling, the first pass in Mexico, the Russian adventure, Thailand, and all the rest of it. Now I'm going to distill all that experience into nine rules or principles for selling. You already know my selling techniques. Remember that we're all selling, we're all selling ourselves as we go through life, so these nine rules are rules for living as well as for selling.

Chapter Eleven

Gayle's Nine "Bes"

You can treat this chapter on my nine "Bes" as a summary of my sales techniques. I've sprinkled it with some reminders of how my work illustrates a sales principle. In some cases I've pulled in examples from the sales experiences of others because I think they are excellent examples.

Why do I have nine selling principles when some books on selling have a dozen, or twenty, or more? One reason is, nine things are easier to remember than twenty. My nine cover all the territory. Another advantage is that you can put all nine "Bes" on a short list in your billfold, purse, IPhone or briefcase, and have them there for ready reference. Of course if you are selling very unusual goods, you will want to consult specialized treatments of your issues, but for selling most items from Cadillacs to Cracker Jacks, these nine will do the job. Besides, the Almighty gave Moses only ten rules, so I'm going to stay out of His league. I've been in real estate so long that most of my examples are drawn from that activity but you can easily transfer them to yours. Here we go.

• • •

One: Be Self Assured. Nobody is going to have any confidence in anything you say or do if you lack self assurance. Self assurance isn't arrogance or condescension. It does not mean presuming to know absolutely everything connected with your business. People pick up arrogance, condescension or pretense right away, no matter how well you try to disguise it. Self assurance means knowing that you have mastered the art of selling as best you can, that you have a proven system for attracting the client to your product, and that you have prepared as best you can to meet as many of the objections to a purchase as you are able. I think that the "gate selling" method is tops and urge you to go back to Chapter Five to review it. If you have a better system, use it. The important thing is that whatever method you choose works best for you.

If you are self assured you can meet any client with confidence. You will meet people who are more intelligent and insightful than you, no matter how bright you think you are. You will meet people with more money than you may ever hope to have. If you are self assured, that won't make any difference because you are in charge of the sales program, you are the one who's asking the questions, you are the one who's showing the property. If you fawn over the smart and the wealthy they will take you for any easy mark and they will walk all over you. It's as bad as condescending or pretending to have perfect knowledge to people you think are dumb.

Another word about the people you may think are not quite bright. Stupid as they may be in your view, they will sense your feeling of superiority and react negatively. In all probability you'll lose a sale, and your client will make sure that all of his friends know that you are an arrogant smarty pants. Meet people on a high level. They will match your level and you will close more sales. One of my woman clients – to whom I sold a house, by the way – remarked that I "Didn't condescend, didn't treat me like a 'little lady,' didn't pat me on the head, didn't talk down to me."

Here is an illustration of what I mean by meeting a customer on a high level. Once when I was in San Francisco I stopped by a shoe store to buy a pair of shoes. The salesman met me on a high level, asking reasonable, friendly questions about why I was in San Francisco. Was I enjoying the scenery, the restaurants, the pretty girls walking around? Sure, he was using a "gate selling" technique, establishing what my needs or desires were, but he wasn't talking up or down to me, and that's my point.

Probably, and I say probably, I had more of the world's possessions, creature comforts, and experiences than he ever would have. Probably he didn't know Eric Berne or Bernie Cornfeld or had been to Paris. He may have been independently wealthy, selling shoes for a lark, but I doubt it. His circumstances or mine made no difference to either of us on that day. He had me try on a pair of $150 shoes, a lot of money for shoes then. "It still is!" you may say, and I agree.

The salesman didn't tell me about the construction of the shoes, their durability, and all that. Instead, in a forthright way that carried authority he said, "Oh, by the way, when you're climbing the hills in San Francisco, and we have some pretty steep hills, these shoes will be so comfortable, and the girls are going to look at them and say 'Wow! Neat pair of shoes!'" Of course I bought the doggone things. In part, that sale was his reward for meeting me on a high level without either fawning or condescending.

Bert is another good example. Years ago Bert lived in a state where a real estate agent had to read a house sale contract to a buyer. Bert once remarked, "You know, with some customers, you sit there and read the contract, and they sit across from you, and you can see their eyes glazing over, and you know that you might as well be reading *Little Bo Peep*." Did Bert really condescend to those clients or any others? Did he assume that he could rush through the contract because the sale was in the bag? No! He was just letting off steam to his audience.

Bert put as much enthusiasm and emphasis into reading that contract as he possibly could. He would break up the reading with comments like, "Now here is a clause I have difficulty explaining because of the legalease, so please ask questions if I'm not making it clear." He told himself that some clients didn't have his educational opportunities, that they lacked his life experience or his expertise. If they'd had his advantages they'd be buying and selling their own real estate. For Bert, reading the contract was just as important a part of the sale as explaining how the bonus room or the water feature in the back yard would enhance the buyer's lifestyle. He assured himself that he could make something as deadly dull as a contract meaningful to his clients.

Self assurance is essential because things are not always going to go your way. Despite your best efforts at meeting stalls or objections to closing, some customers won't close and you'll lose a sale. You can't control the economic cycle. Recessions are going to happen as sure as sunrise. You can meliorate the economic downturns by following all of my principles, but sales will be fewer. You are going to have your own down days when you don't feel like putting forth the effort. If you have self assurance, though, you will go on to the next customer, the next turn of the economic wheel, or the next day with strong self confidence.

All right, how do you get and keep self assurance? Good question. I wish I knew the absolute answer. If I did, I'd bottle self assurance, sell it for a handsome profit, and be sitting behind the CEO's desk of a multibillion dollar corporation. My alternate advice is to read *How To Win Friends and Influence People* or *Think and Grow Rich*, not once but again and again. Apply their rules and constantly measure how well you are doing. Or take a course from Success Motivation International, complete the course, and check your progress toward the goals laid out there. Better yet, do all three. Whatever you do, persevere in your reading or course taking even after you begin to see good results. You can never have too much self assurance.

• • •

Two: Be Honest. Does this admonition make you tired? Be honest, now. It makes me tired, too. There's so much emphasis on honesty that you sometimes think that books on selling are really scouting manuals or kindergarten stories. Why the obsession with honesty? Because it's so easy to be dishonest when a sale is at stake. Sure, there are laws and regulations and codes of ethics, but a determined agent can slither around them for years without getting any more than a slap on the wrist. We all know those people.

In one U.S. city an agent didn't reveal hidden defects in houses and did other shady things. He made sales. The new owners threatened to sue until they found out that the costs of a suit would be about the cost of repairs, so instead they complained to the president of the real estate company. The president called in the offending agent and said, "Naughty, naughty, mustn't do."

Guess what? The agent went right back on the street and did the same thing again. After several years of buyers' complaints to the state licensing board, his license was revoked. Meanwhile he'd made a good living, in part by shading the truth. Of course he eventually lost his job, was disgraced, and had to find other work.

It's better not to get started down that road. Honesty is its own reward.

Sometimes honesty is rewarded very well. Gloria is an agent in a southwestern state where it's warm and wet enough to encourage subterranean termites. She got a call from an owner who wanted to list his house, a two-story A frame. Gloria went to the property, a small acreage on a paved road near a reservoir lake. Oaks, cedars, and hackberrys grew right up to the little clearing surrounding the house. The lake and the trees cooled the temperature at least fifteen degrees, a welcome relief on that blistering hot day. After Gloria walked over the land and through the attractive house, the owner admitted to a little problem, one Gloria already suspected. Termites infested those solid-looking A beams.

Gloria tried reasoning with the owner to make repairs. He said no. She pointed out that an inspector hired by a buyer would find the termites and then he'd either have to make repairs or drop the price. He said that not every buyer hired an inspector. She cited a state law requiring an extermination by a state-licensed exterminator at the time of the sale. The exterminator would, she said, discover the infestation and note it on his report. The owner replied that maybe the buyer wouldn't read the report. Gloria listed the property because it was so inviting, but resolved to level with prospective buyers about the termites.

Gloria's first client was a woman who was looking for a house for herself, her husband and their son. She fell in love with the house and grounds and wanted to close right away, without an inspection. Gloria told the woman about the termites, lost the sale, and eventually delisted the property because the owner was so uncooperative. But her client was impressed with Gloria's honesty. She asked Gloria to find a good house in the same area. Gloria sold the family a nearby property even better suited to them, received her commission, and everybody was happy. She would have been satisfied with doing the right thing by warning her client about the termites but in this instance her honesty really paid off.

Of course you can't honestly reveal something you don't know about. If you do know about a visible defect or an obvious problem there's no need to undermine a sale by harping on it. If a house needs repainting, any fool can see that. Mention it clearly and emphatically, and move on to the positives.

Here's an example from my own experience. When I was selling lots in Lomas del Centenario, occasionally a buyer would ask about earthquakes. Were there earthquakes here? I said no because I'd never heard of one. Then we had an earthquake. It shook us around a little but didn't hurt anyone or damage anything. "Oops, I'll have to revise my spiel," I told my colleagues. I did revise it, but I didn't dwell on earthquakes or any other negative. In both cases, before and after the earthquakes, I made honest statements based on my knowledge at the time.

• • •

Three: Be Appropriately Dressed. Find out what is correct for wear in your community and wear it. If you think that what is accepted dress is too formal or too casual, you are welcome to your opinion, but wear it anyway. Be a trend-setter or express your individuality in some other area of your life. Be aware, too, that what is appropriate for one phase or activity isn't necessarily appropriate for another. To mention one obvious example, even the best beachwear isn't going to cut it at the debutante ball.

I told my classes, "Dress inconspicuously, dress so nobody notices your clothes." That was, and is, good advice. The trick is to anticipate what is inconspicuous under any and all circumstances. I didn't always learn those niceties as quickly as I could have. Here are some good lessons from my experience.

In Cabo San Lucas there was never a problem with ultra-casual style. I was a salesman, and if a salesman wore anything fancier than shorts, a T-shirt, and sandals he risked losing business on account of his perceived snootiness. Everybody expected extreme informality and, believe me, it was a pleasure to comply. In Acapulco, in sales situations, it was much the same. My everyday selling and office wear was shorts, a shirt with collar, low-slung shoes and low-cut socks. Acapulco was a little more formal, so there were occasions such as office parties where it was acceptable to wear long pants.

What I forgot in Acapulco was that I wasn't just a salesman

any longer, I was also the project director. Now I had a secretary, Maria, who was a first rate assistant, spoke fluent English, and had a wicked sense of humor. I'll get to my learning experiences in a moment, but first I want to brag on Maria's intelligence and cleverness. I noticed right away that Maria, for all her good qualities, had a messy desk. She piled stacks of paper, small boxes, yesterday's lunch, and what-have-you here and there. She could always find anything she needed in those piles, so her untidiness was not a practical issue.

On the other hand, I kept my desk neat to the point of sweeping it clean every evening. I'd dump unfinished work in drawers just to get it off my desk. So I thought I'd be smarty about her untidy

My wonderful secretary, Maria, and I are clowning for the camera. Maria was an excellent secretary, efficient, fluent in English, and possessed a wicked sense of humor. At my encouragement, she later moved into sales, where she became a top closer of the townhouse business.

desk. One day I came in early and left a note, "A cluttered desk is a sign of a cluttered mind." Ha, ha, I'd been so cute. The next morning I arrived a little after Maria. She greeted me but didn't mention my note. When I went to my otherwise bare desk, there was a note in her handwriting: "If a cluttered desk is a sign of a cluttered mind, what's an empty desk the sign of?"

That was Maria.

But I was telling you about my lack of dress code sense. It happened that we were having trouble getting our phone system installed. With every delay the more our construction advanced, and the more difficult and expensive it became to insert the wiring into the walls. It fell to me to break the logjam, so Maria talked to the secretary of the manager of the local phone system. The other guy's secretary kept putting us off with stories about how busy and important her boss was. Finally Maria convinced the other secretary that I was busy and important too.

After Maria got our appointment, we left for the manager's office, Maria going along as my interpreter, and me dressed in my shirt, shorts, shoes and socks. I was neatly dressed – you can look neat wearing anything – but definitely I was casual. We went into the head man's office and met him. We negotiated, reached an agreement, drew up the papers, initialed all the pages, put them down, and the business part of the meeting was over.

Everything seemed to be fine. The manager ordered coffee. I could see that he was looking at my legs, and he said something to Maria. She said something back. They both laughed. We chatted a little, drank the coffee, and left with the usual formal Mexican goodbyes. Maria and I had a conversation about the last part of the meeting as we went down the stairs and strolled out of the building.

"Maria," I said, "I couldn't help but notice that you and the manager were talking and joking and looking at my knobby knees. What was that all about?"

"He said, 'If he's such an important man, why does he wear shorts to a business meeting?'"

"What did you say?"

"I told him you were eccentric."

After that I wore long pants to all business meetings.

Following the lesson from Maria, I raised my antenna on the dress issue, and found it much easier to get along if I dressed appropriately. I recalled that my boss, the developer, told me to wear a suit when visiting the president of Mexico. Probably he hadn't trusted my sense of propriety. I was embarrassed enough that I always dressed correctly when working out of our offices in Mexico City, where at least a coat, tie, and slacks were the minimum business dress. I lived in the Zona Rosa, then one of the most fashionable areas of the capital, and scarcely ever appeared on the street without wearing acceptable clothes.

• • •

Four: Be Friendly, for the purpose of making friends. Of course you're going to be friendly. You'll leave personal upsets behind when you meet clients. You'll be cheerful despite the fact that your spouse ran into the garage door frame while putting away the car, your sixteen-year-old promised to mow the lawn and didn't, and the cat vomited on the Persian carpet. But I mean more than that. I mean make friends even if you don't make a sale. If I had to choose, sure, I'd rather make a sale because I've gotten into the bad habit of using some of my commission income for eating. Most of the time you can do both, if you remember that making a friend is the next best thing to making a sale.

Friendships are among the most valuable human coin in the world. I can't tell you how many times friends have helped me in large ways and small. I've tried to reciprocate and always found it a joy to do so. I emphasize this because often the way to make a friend is to spend more time with a client than is absolutely necessary to make a sale. I do that because almost everybody has an interest or a hobby I know nothing of, but would like to learn more about. I'm on the go so much that I don't have the time to read or to watch documentaries as often as I'd like.

I learn a lot from friendly conversations with clients, after I've made my pitch and shown them the properties that I want to show them. You may think that some hobbies, such as studying butterflies or restoring Model A Fords are crashing bores, but if they are what fascinates a client, listen to their stories in a friendly way. You may discover that any pastime that excites a fellow human is worth knowing about. This is especially true if you later have another client who's interested in butterflies or Model A Fords. Then you can impress that client by asking intelligent questions.

Let me tell you about a favor a friend did for me. One day the town of El Centenario shut off our water for a day and a half, either to repair a pipe or to make some improvement. My friend lived in Ed Rose's development, Lomas del Centenario, where there is a separate water system. He brought me three two-and-a-half gallon jugs of water. That little gesture gave me enough water for cooking, refilling toilets, and for watering Dolly, my dog, and Boots, my cat. It was a small thing, one I appreciated not so much for itself, but because he thought enough about my situation to respond to it. Good friendships often are made up of such gestures. And, did I mention that I'd sold his house to him?

• • •

Five: Be Generous. This "Be" is closely tied to being a friend. Nobody likes a tightwad or skinflint, the type who counts every penny, feeds his guests and clients cheap meals, whines about his expenses and high cost of living, and stiffs servers in restaurants. That kind of conduct drives people away, in part because they assume that miserliness masks other unpleasant traits. If you are generous the added expenses will come back to you through increased sales.

By "generous" I don't mean being open-handed, an easy mark, or a soft touch for clients who want loans. If they try any of that you have to tell them, in a gentle, reasonable way, that you aren't able to do any more than you are doing. Showing them around town, buying their meals, or allowing them to stay free of charge in my guest house are reasonable, in my view. People appreciate considerations like that. They feel friendly toward you even if you don't close with them.

• • •

Six: Be Early. Try to be early for appointments, even if you have to wait in your car for a few minutes or longer than a few minutes. Most books on selling will tell you to be on time but being early is better. Here's why: some people naturally think that it's better to be early than late, and they're not going to change their habits because they have an appointment with you. So they'll turn up early and wonder where you are.

Here's another reason: people set their watches differently, say no more than two to five minutes in most cases. If they have traveled through a time zone to meet you, they may make a small mistake when they set their watches forward or back, maybe for those two to five minutes. If a customer waits two to five minutes, though, that's an eternity to him. He'll figure that you really don't care to sell him anything because you aren't showing him enough respect to be on time.

You may be thinking, "Well, gosh, it's all very fine to preach about being early but I don't have enough hours in the day as it is. I don't want to waste time sitting around in my car waiting for somebody to show up." Hold on! Did I mention anything about wasting time? No!

I'll illustrate the point with David, who's an agent specializing in house sales and subdivision development. He's a Civil War buff who arrives early, taking along a book on some leader, unit, battle, campaign, or political aspect of the Civil War. He reads the book until his client appears. You may think that it's a waste of time to read so much as one line about the Civil War because crocheting is your thing. OK, bring along that sweater or tea towel you're working on. While I'm waiting I read my schedule for the day and check my client list to see if I've missed anything that I should be doing with or about any of them. Which brings me to –

• • •

Seven: Be Aggressive in keeping track of clients. Have a system for developing prospects or making cold calls, those phone calls or house visits in which you say, "Hi, I'm Sam Brown, would you like to sell you house or do you know any neighbors who would?" Have a system for staying in touch with people you've already sold. If you made them happy with their sales, they are among your best prospects for a resale of their house or referring other clients to you. Or maybe you didn't sell them on the first effort, but they're possible future buyers. Stop in to visit with them, too. There are so many systems or combinations of systems out there that I won't try to describe them. Any agent or company you work with can suggest some or show you theirs.

My system is old fashioned but it works for me. I have 3" x 5" cards in a recipe box and a Rolodex. My grandkids say, "Grandad, where's your BlackBerry?" I have three cell phones. One is for local calls and for calling the United States when I have to, because the Telmex phone system blocks out-of-country calls that don't use their phones. The other is for use when I'm in the U.S. The third keeps me in direct touch with my office.

Mostly, though, I use e-mail. I keep my computer up to date and my backup current. Almost every past, present, or potential buyer has an active e-mail and the great thing about e-mail is that it's international. Sometimes I'll select a client and send them what amounts to "Hello, how are you? Remember me?" If I hear or read a good joke that's not offensive in any way I'll send it out to everyone in my e-mail address book. That move always brings at least a few replies. It's a good way to stay in touch.

• • •

Eight: Be Alert to opportunities in all situations, including the most unlikely. Being alert to opportunities outside the box of your immediate circumstances is, to me, the toughest challenge in selling. I think that great sellers are made, not born, and that one key to being a great seller is being alert to related opportunities. A person can know all the rules of "gate selling" and apply them, absorb and apply my principles or anyone else's, do absolutely everything correctly, and never exploit a collateral opportunity that will pay off in a big way. The best advice I can give is this: always be ready to follow up on a bold idea that comes to you, no matter how crazy or wacky you or others think it is at the time.

My most personally satisfying coup was selling that penthouse to the wife of the president of Mexico. Why did I take along those photos of our development models? I don't know, except that I sensed her displeasure over the phone and subconsciously believed that the photos might mollify her over the gift to "That Woman." Then there was my making friends with the man whose car I rear-ended, the sheriff of King County, Washington. That took some brass, I admit, and my gesture might have gone nowhere. But it did go somewhere in a way that I couldn't anticipate, selling all those Fords to Boeing.

My colleagues ridiculed the idea of selling those reconfigured VW bugs to Volkswagen dealers to display alongside their unmodified beetles. They thought the dealers would never spring for such a crazy idea. But the dealers did. My Costamex bosses recoiled at my idea of switching from condo to timeshare sales. I believed what I was proposing was right, and was willing to spend some of my own money to go on leave, learn the timeshare business, and come back with a written report on timesharing. Eventually they concluded that I was right, and I made back much more than my expenses.

There's no formula for exploiting opportunities, it's just a matter of quick, bold thinking, determination, and belief in yourself and your product. The books and courses won't tell you how to do it. I don't know how to do it, either, except that when the light bulb lit up in my head, I followed through. There's no question but what there were opportunities out there that I never developed. I can't tell you what they were because I never thought of them. So I'll leave you with my final advice on this subject, be alert to opportunities and seize them.

• • •

Nine: Be Confident. Well, I began with Be Self Assured and I'm ending with Be Confident. Aren't they the same thing? No. Being self assured is believing in yourself. Being confident is believing in the environment you're working in, in your bosses and subordinates, and in your company. If I hadn't had confidence in my uncle, Eugene Wagner, or in Ford cars, I'd have left my first sales job long before I did.

Did I think that we had the only good dealership in the Seattle area? Of course not. I'd never argue with a customer about the relative merits of dealerships. Instead I'd mention our great combination of a large selection of cars, favorable pricing and terms, and service.

Did I think that Fords were the only decent cars on the road? Again, of course not. If a customer said he'd been looking at Chevrolets, I didn't say, "Oh, Chevys stink," and get into one of those interminable, unwinnable debates over the strengths and weaknesses of different makes. Rather, I'd point out the advantages of the Ford, like the safety door locks.

The same goes for all the other companies I'd headed up or worked for. I never had an occasion to distrust a company or most co-workers. Naturally, I liked some people better than others. Then there was Evan, the guy the Russian Mafia turned. But believe me, if I had lost confidence in a company or its workforce in general, I'd have been out the door. One thing I learned through a friend's experience was that one bad apple doesn't spoil a company. This story is more than a little troubling, so you may want to skip it and go on to my last example of the results of confidence.

The troubling story concerns my friend Kenny, who worked with me for some time in Costamex. Kenny wasn't impressive looking. He was a big guy, over six feet tall, but a bit overweight and a chain smoker. He had positive qualities, though. He was determined to see every problem through to a constructive solution. He was a first rate detail man, and an excellent accountant. He was very good at keeping track of things that others are likely to overlook or forget about while a company grows and spreads out over a large number of offices. After a few years of moving around Mexico, he went back to Cabo San Lucas for a short stay, remembered how much he'd liked it before, and decided to remain.

Kenny went to work for a much smaller but very active company there in Cabo. I visited him once. He told me, "We've got this new guy in the office." Just then the man strolled into the room, he and Kenny smiled at each other, and the man left. He wasn't a salesman, he was a chauffeur and all-round gofer.

"I don't like that guy," Kenny continued. "He came in one day, asked for the job and got it. He's always watching everything, looking at me, and I know he knows I make the bank deposits." On a typical day, as the new man observed, Kenny gathered up the receipts at the close of business, took them to his house, then deposited them the next day after the bank opened.

This routine continued for a while, with the gofer carefully studying Kenny's habits. He also learned that Kenny had a collection of antique guns including handguns. Handgun ownership is highly restricted in Mexico, but these were guns for display and for their extrinsic value, not for use. Handguns are so restricted that only the army, the police, and, naturally, the criminals and the gangs have handguns.

One night the gofer and a sidekick of his broke into Kenny's house, armed with handguns, of course. They trussed him up with cord, so that his hands and feet were tied together behind his back. They slapped duct tape across his mouth and threw him into the bathtub, face down. He lay in the bathtub on his belly for two days, the cord biting into his wrists and ankles, cutting off his circulation. The gofer and his pal left with Kenny's gun collection and his bank deposits. Kenny lived a ways out of town so nobody heard the commotion.

When those couple of days went by and Kenny didn't show up at work, his associates got curious and sent an office boy over to check on him. The kid stood outside yelling, "Kenny, Kenny." No answer. Kenny was finally able to squirm around a little and bang his feet on the tub. The kid forced the door, found him, untied him, and the company flew him to a specialist in Mexico City. The specialist worked on his wrists and hands, ankles and feet, and restored the circulation. The specialist remarked, "If you had been one hour later, we would have had to amputate his hands." Kenny was tough or he wouldn't have survived. He was in rehab a long time as it was.

The rest of the story, as they say, was that Kenny had a good friend in the federal police. The federal policeman traced the gofer and his buddy up the highway to La Paz, found that they'd taken the ferry across the Gulf of California to Mazatlán, and were enjoying life in that famous resort. He went to Mazatlán, was gone a few days, then returned to Cabo San Lucas.

"Let's go have lunch," he said to Kenny.

At lunch he explained: "The job is taken care of. You'll be glad to know those two guys had a very long, slow, painful death. They won't be bothering you again. We took care of them. I have some photos. Would you care to see them?" Kenny declined.

The point of this grisly story is that Kenny could have blamed the company for hiring such a bad man. He could have quit in a huff. He might have sued. Instead he remembered the co-workers who wondered where he was, the office boy who broke in to find him, and the company's flying him to the specialist in Mexico City. He stayed with the company until he died of a heart attack unrelated to his ordeal.

My last story about confidence involves my wonderful secretary, Maria. I had complete confidence in her. Often I'd say to her, "As good as you are, you ought to be in sales." Finally she took my advice, moved to the Cancun operation of Costamex, and made about ten times as much money closing timeshare sales. I lost a top secretary but the company gained a great seller.

• • •

There you have it. Please remember my nine principles: be self assured, be honest, be appropriately dressed, be friendly for the purpose of making friends, be generous, be early for appointments, be aggressive in keeping touch with clients, be alert to opportunities, and be confident. Good luck to you!

Breinigsville, PA USA
08 March 2011
257184BV00002B/2/P

9 781934 95634